the UPS and DOWNS of running a small business

LESSONS ON LIFE, FAMILY, AND ENTREPRENEURSHIP

JAMES F. COMLEY *with Jason R. Rich*

Broad Book Studio, an imprint of Broad Book Press

Paperback ISBN: 978-1963549386
eBook ISBN: 9781963549393
Published and printed in the United States.
Library of Congress Control Number: 2025922940

Contents

Introduction

AS I BEGAN WORK on this book, I lived through yet another major milestone—my 95th birthday. Looking back, during my nine-and-a-half decades of life, I came to the realization that I've experienced a lot. I consider myself truly lucky, because in addition to my health, I've been part of an incredibly close family. This includes the relationship and life I built with Virginia, my wife of over 66 years.

Before she passed away in November 2019, not only did she and I raise four children (who are now successful adults), we were able to see our grandchildren and great grandchildren become a cherished part of our extended family. My wife was my partner in every sense of the world. She was my support system in life, both at home and in business.

Since 1972, when my business partner, John L. McHugh, and I took over Woburn, Massachusetts-based Embree Elevator (www.embreeelevator.com), I have been the driving force responsible for taking a small business and transforming it into an extremely successful family business that operates throughout Eastern Massachusetts and Southern New Hampshire. For much of my time with Embree Elevator, my wife served as a founding partner, bookkeeper, and secretary.

My family has been in the elevator industry for four generations. I am proud that my business continues to support several generations of my own family, and multiple generations of our employees. And while I remain the President/CEO of the company, it's now my daughter Carol and her husband Cliff who handle the business' day-to-day operations.

While I feel extremely blessed to have accomplished so much during my time on this planet, I do not consider my success in life or business to be a result of luck alone. It took many years of persistence—working six days a week, often 10 or more hours per day.

Yet, because I was doing something I enjoyed, and had the support of my loved ones, much of what I did day-to-day, year-after-year was driven by true passion, hard work, dedication, and my ability to stay motivated (even during the most difficult times). The skills I developed around building strong and lasting business relationships was also a key to my success.

Earlier in my life, my goal was to retire comfortably at age 40, which is something I could easily have done. Yet, because of my love for work, I have yet to experience true retirement (although I no longer go into the office more than a few times per month).

I graduated from high school in 1948 and then went to trade school to become a licensed electrician. I never attended college. As a result, I did not formally study business, accounting, management, entrepreneurship, marketing, or any of the other skillsets that are typically required to run a business. I learned by doing and by staying true to my core philosophies which I plan to share with you, the reader.

The management style that I first started to develop more than 57 years ago (when I founded my first company) has evolved over time but is still successfully being implemented. You see, I have always been a firm believer in developing strong and mutually beneficial relationships with my employees, customers, and suppliers.

I wholeheartedly believe it's my ability to build and grow these relationships based on mutual respect, trust, and honest in-person communication that has allowed me and my business to establish and maintain unique relationships that have resulted in many of my employees, customers, and suppliers being loyal to me and my company.

Yes, business is about making money, taking risks, and pursuing growth, but I have learned first hand that it can be so much more than that. I have put a lot of importance on safety, relationships, supporting those around me, and on giving back to my country, industry, and community.

While I have learned to delegate responsibilities over the years, I have never been someone who stays confined to an office. Even once I had many employees working for me, I never hesitated to answer a service call at 3:00 am or go to a work site to meet with customers in-person or help an employee complete a difficult job. In other words, my life has never been about working a 9:00 am to 5:00 pm job.

However, I always tried to make it home for dinner and spend Sundays with my family. Even during the busiest and most stressful times working as a business operator, maintaining a work/life balance always remained a top priority. This is a core reason I now have such a close-knit family.

I have always tried to maintain a positive attitude and good sense of humor. My goal has always been to learn something new every day. And equally important, I've strived to maintain an open line of communication with all of my family members, employees, customers, suppliers, people in the International Union of Elevator Constructors (IUEC), and those in my industry and community.

I am a strong believer in having mentors to learn from and serving as a mentor to help others. I have also discovered firsthand that having a strong work ethic, using common sense, and making smart financial decisions are keys to success—regardless of what industry you work in, where you live, or what job title you hold.

The Ups and Downs of Running a Small Business is not an autobiography. I am writing this book to serve as an educational tool to assist people who are first entering the workforce, and those who have an entrepreneurial spirit and plan to start their own business venture.

While I have served as a one-on-one mentor to my children, grandchildren, some of my employees, people in my industry, and a variety of people I have met throughout the past few decades, I am writing this book to pay it forward and share my knowledge, experiences, and advice with you—just as a mentor would.

The business world has certainly changed a lot over the past few decades, but the information and philosophies I plan to share with you are timeless and can apply to almost anyone, regardless of their job title or industry. Let's face it, many people don't have a 95-year-old business person who can share their wisdom and advice. This is what I hope to do here for you.

All of the business philosophies, practices, beliefs, and experiences I plan to share have worked for me. Feel free to pick and choose what information applies to your situation and that resonates with you, so you can benefit from my knowledge and experiences. And hopefully, you can avoid some of the mistakes I've made during my own professional journey.

In today's busy world that's dominated by fast-evolving technologies, including artificial intelligence, it's vital to stay informed, continue to learn, expand your skillset, and maintain a positive outlook to help ensure a successful personal and professional future. In many situations, you cannot fight change, but you can learn to adapt without compromising your principles, ethics, or reputation.

I am a strong believer in building a support system, only taking calculated risks, focusing on maintaining open and honest communication, and always looking out for the safety and well-being of those around me—including my employees, customers, and the general public.

These days, people all over the world ride in elevators and never think twice about the experience. That's because people know elevators, escalators, and people movers are now perfectly safe—for those who build them, maintain them, and who are passengers on them. This was not always the case, however.

On both a state and federal level, I have worked tirelessly for the elevator industry to adopt strict safety standards. For example, I invested more than 20 years (including four years as Chairman) serving on the Massachusetts Board of Elevator Regulations in the state's Department of Public Safety. This has been a passion of mine since early in my career, and something I have invested thousands of hours into on a voluntary basis.

While some people volunteer to help save the whales, protect our environment, or help those in need, my philanthropic work has often been to make elevators, escalators, and people movers as safe as possible.

Looking back, I am very proud that my work has led to changes in how elevators are designed, built, and maintained. It's work that has literally saved lives and made it possible for people to ride elevators and escalators without having to worry about getting injured or killed.

Through the time I spent in the United States Navy, between 1951 and 1955 aboard the USS Hawkins, and through travel I have done with my family, I have had the opportunity to visit many places around the world. I've experienced numerous cultures, interacted with people from all walks of life, and learned a lot from people with vastly different perspectives.

I have loved the adventures I have taken throughout the world but have also learned that there's no place I'd rather live than within the United States of America. I am proud of my country, honored to have served to protect it, and wholeheartedly believe that supporting U.S. businesses is essential.

This is why my company continues to rely on parts and equipment made in America, despite it being possible to spend less and make more profit if we were to use foreign-made parts and equipment that are often substandard.

One thing you'll learn from me is that I am a strong believer in patriotism, the importance of unions for protecting American workers, and safety—which for me, are more important than profit. And while you may think this way of thinking can be counterproductive, it's gone a long way toward helping me build my reputation and then grow and maintain a successful business that's been in operation under my leadership for more than 56 years.

It's my hope that by sharing my experiences, insight, knowledge, and philosophies, you will be able to adapt this information in a way that can help build your own career and perhaps your own business.

During my 95 years, I have experienced success and happiness, and some devastating personal and professional losses which I've had to overcome. As you embark on your own career, you too can expect many ups and downs, successes and failures, personal wins, and heart-wrenching losses. This is all what makes life worth living.

Along the way, if you can learn from others, you're willing to work hard, at times make a few sacrifices, and take some calculated (not careless) risks, there's no stopping you from achieving your own dreams and professional aspirations. I am living proof of this.

WHAT YOU CAN EXPECT FROM THIS BOOK

Throughout this book, I will be sharing important life lessons I've learned over the past 95 years—relating to family, friends, achieving happiness and fulfillment, and maintaining a strong work ethic.

I will emphasize several principles relating to perseverance, service, loyalty, honesty, and passion in many ways. And ultimately, I will share 25 core philosophies that I have lived by, and that have helped me achieve happiness and success—with very few regrets along the way. This starts with a motto I've always lived by—"Every day is a good day, but some days are better than others." I'll talk more about why this concept resonates so strongly with me a bit later.

Many business books focus on teaching basic concepts. What sets *The Ups and Downs of Running a Small Business* apart is that what you're about to read is based on my actual life and professional experiences. I have learned by doing. The information herein is knowledge I have acquired first-hand, and that's helped me achieve success. Now, it's time for me to pass this knowledge to the next generation of entrepreneurs.

So, whether you're first graduating from high school, college, or a trade school, you're hoping to advance your career working for your current employer, plan to break into a new industry, or ultimately want to launch your own business, it's my sincere hope that what you learn by reading *The Ups and Downs of Running a Small Business* will be helpful in all aspects of your life, and especially your career.

HOW THIS BOOK CAME ABOUT

The concept for *The Ups and Downs of Running a Small Business* was the brainchild of my daughter Bonnie, who is a successful entrepreneur in her own right as the founder and CEO of BroadwayHD, and a variety of other theatrical endeavors.

While Bonnie did not ultimately join the family business (Embree

Elevator), for her entire life she's been privy to seeing my entrepreneurial spirit at work. She credits some of her success to mimicking my drive, passion, work ethic, and business philosophies—with a focus on building community. Here she is in her words describing my commitment to creating something that goes beyond the borders of a town:

"Not every entrepreneur aspires to build the next Amazon or Walmart. A small, local business can provide a meaningful livelihood for decades, supporting families, strengthening communities, and creating lasting impact far beyond its geographic footprint. The neighborhood hair salon, the bakery that makes every birthday cake, the pizza shop that celebrates Little League victories, these businesses may serve a single town, but their influence endures in the lives they touch," Bonnie said. And she's right—those elements of community matter, and have mattered to me, always.

She went on to talk about my legacy. Her words are special, and mean so much to me, as I have worked hard to leave a lasting impact on my family, community, and industry. She said, "My father's elevator company operated in one region of New England, yet his impact reached far beyond it. Through his deep expertise in elevator mechanics, he volunteered his time to help shape safety manuals and industry regulations. Though his business was local, his contributions to elevator safety have helped prevent injuries, save lives, and protect property worldwide, proving that even a small business rooted in one community can make a global difference. I think his advice in this book will inspire and guide others to walk the same path as business owners."

Anyway, once Bonnie came up with the concept for this book, she and I sat down numerous times to flesh out the ideas in a way that would be of interest to the masses—not just those in the elevator industry. After a lot of back and forth, this is an objective I believe we've accomplished.

Since I was not about to sit for countless hours in front of my computer trying to actually write a full-length book, I began dictating my ideas and memories into a recorder. And since I am a firm believer that, when it's appropriate, it's a good strategy to delegate work to people I trust and who often have a different skillset, the next step was to partner with an experienced journalist and author to help me.

This author and I then spent over 30 hours doing one-on-one interviews in my home. He was instrumental in organizing my ideas and content into a cohesive manuscript.

So, in the vein of total transparency, what you're reading are all my ideas, based on my experiences, knowledge, memories, and business philosophies. It was my daughter and journalist Jason Rich who took this information and formulated it into a viable manuscript, which was then turned over to the publisher. What you're holding in your hands is the end result of a group effort, and something I am proud to share.

1
I've Learned So Much in 95 Years

"Being an entrepreneur means working 80 hours a week to avoid working 40 for someone else."

LORI GREINER

THERE ARE a few important lessons I've learned after more than 70 years as a business operator. And if you plan to follow in my footsteps, pursue your entrepreneurial spirit, and potentially start your own business, you need to go into it understanding several things.

WHAT BEING AN ENTREPRENEUR AND BUSINESS OWNER REALLY MEANS

First, being an entrepreneur is not a job or career. It's a lifestyle. One that requires you to take on many responsibilities and be able to juggle them without allowing anything to fall through the cracks. It's about trusting and believing in yourself, knowing how to interact with others, and staying true to your vision.

For me, it's also been about maintaining a positive attitude and sense of humor, regardless of what's happening in my own life or around me.

Being an entrepreneur and business operator is not a 9:00am to 5:00pm job where you only work Mondays through Fridays. You can't always take holidays off or go on vacations whenever you please. It's about making decisions, taking calculated risks, and being able to stay motivated (even during difficult times).

I've also discovered that being a business owner sometimes requires having to deal with difficult people. Understanding how to avoid (or at least overcome) conflict is an important skill. I've worked hard over the years to maintain the trust and respect of my employees, customers, suppliers, bankers, accountants, lawyers, and countless other people whom I interacted with professionally.

Taking on the role of founder and CEO of a business also requires making intelligent financial decisions. It's about knowing when and how to grow and expand, and determining when to change strategies, or adopt new business practices to keep things moving forward in a positive way.

Knowing that your actions, decisions, and leadership skills have a direct impact on your personal finances, and the financial wellbeing of your family and your employees (and their families), is also an ongoing responsibility that you must take seriously.

As part of this self-imposed set of responsibilities, I've always believed wholeheartedly in keeping my employees and customers safe, even when it is not necessarily in the company's best financial interest to do so. Yes, my goal has always been to make money, be profitable, and grow my company, but there have always been many exceptions to this way of thinking.

It's essential to understand the impact of growth, and how it can positively or negatively change the lives of the people you're ultimately responsible for. I think I did a good job growing fast enough to keep up with the times, but slow enough that we never lost control over the business or its goals.

I saw several competitors throughout the decades try to grow too fast. They wound up hiring people who were not qualified to do the work and didn't invest the time to properly train them. Instead, they spent a lot of money buying new company trucks and fancy gear to keep up appearances, but they could not do the work properly. As a result, those companies wound up failing.

This worked out well for me, because after those companies failed, I was able to buy some of their equipment at a very good price. No matter what type of business you're in, trying to grow too quickly is often a huge and costly mistake.

Sometimes, to get new customers, you have to be the lowest bidder for the job. While you might land that job, there is often not enough money in the budget to then do the work properly. This often means winding up with an unhappy customer and a poor reputation.

If you're seeking out government contractors, for example, you need to be the low bidder. But as the leader of a company making the bid, you have to consider the value of landing the new customer and determine if it makes financial sense moving forward. In other words, it's not always a good idea to take shortcuts as part of your strategy for growing a business.

On top of all this, an entrepreneur must truly understand their business, its purpose, goals, and clientele. Part of this means understanding how the company you operate differentiates itself from its competitors, and how it fits within its industry and the marketplace. The company must fill a need that customers or clients are willing to pay for. There must be enough demand to keep your business profitable.

Thus, having a deep understanding of the industry you're in, your competitors, and the challenges your industry as a whole is facing is essential. Staying informed and being able to make educated predictions about what the future holds is a necessity, too. Over the decades, the technology used in elevators, for example, has evolved a lot. I have always loved learning about everything that's new and then choosing how to adopt the latest technologies and innovations.

I'd love to be able to say that being an entrepreneur and business operator is something that anyone can do. I do not believe this is always the case, however. Many people would love to be their own boss, but don't have the personality or wherewithal to handle the stress, manage the responsibilities, and live the entrepreneurial lifestyle.

Anyone can learn the basics of running a business, but developing an entrepreneurial spirit is not something that can be taught, nor can it be learned from a class or book. I believe it's an intangible thing that you need to find and harness within yourself.

The reason I refer to being an entrepreneur as a lifestyle goes beyond what makes up the workday. It's also about making sacrifices that can (and often does) impact your personal life. This is why I believe it's critical to have the full support of your spouse or partner, and the understanding of your children.

Everyone close to you needs to be on board and understand what's required of you as a business operator. This applies when working in any type of business or industry.

BUSINESS OPERATORS NEED FAMILY SUPPORT

My wife and family have always been my support system. At the same time, I have always done my absolute best to be there for them. Over the years, I unfortunately missed countless sports games, recitals, and activities when my children were young. However, I tried my best to teach them what it means to be a business owner and about the responsibilities that came with it. And whenever possible, I would be home for dinner with my family. I also tried to keep Sundays free to attend church and be with my wife and kids.

Virginia (my wife) fully understood and supported me whenever the phone rang at 3:00am, and I had to go to an emergency job to repair an elevator. She also understood when on countless occasions, I had to work late and miss dinner or forgo the chance to spend quality time with my family to deal with a work-related situation.

Was this easy for any of us? Absolutely not. But over the years, I worked extremely hard to build and maintain close-knit relationships—not just with my wife and children, but with my extended family, too. If my family did not fully support my entrepreneurial spirit and drive to be my own boss and run a business, I could never have achieved success. This was a team effort every step of the way.

So, if you're considering launching your own business, make sure you have the support of your family. Without that support, I believe you'll be fighting an uphill battle on both the work and family fronts, and you will face many additional challenges.

I'll focus more on the importance of my family's support in the next chapter. Plus, you'll read interviews with my daughter and son-in-law who now run the day-to-day operation of Embree Elevator.

I was born during the Great Depression and have always lived in Bedford, Massachusetts. My family was lucky in that my father was able to find work as an electrician, so we never went hungry. He did, however, need to work seven days a week for several years to keep food on the table for myself, my two siblings, and my mother. Back then, he was able to earn $25 per week, but that was enough for us to get by.

Seeing him work so hard helped me understand what it means to have a strong work ethic, even as a young child. Just as my parents taught me the value of having a strong work ethic and the importance of having a close-knit and supportive family, from these interviews with my own kids, you'll discover how I have been able to pass these important values down to two more generations, and how they've flourished with this knowledge.

What I've described thus far just scratches the surface of what it takes to start, maintain, and ultimately grow a business, especially one that remains profitable for decades, and ultimately attracts family members to become a part of it.

Of course, I always wanted my children to grow up and join the family business, but I never insisted on this. I continue to support the decisions my children (who are now adults) and grandchildren have made and encourage them to pursue their own interests. I am proud of what my children and grandchildren have accomplished in their lives thus far and cherish them all.

My core life strategies have been to enjoy life, pursue my passions, build a strong family, avoid having regrets, and to live by the motto, "Every day is a good day—but some days are better than others."

What does this mean to me? Well, it means truly believing that life is good, and that whatever happens, you need to keep going. Enjoy what you have. For me, it also means maintaining a positive attitude and sense of humor, without compromising the strong work ethic that was instilled in me by my father.

LIVING TO 95 TAKES MORE THAN GOOD GENES AND LUCK

Many people ask how I've managed to live to age 95, stay healthy, run a successful business, and be part of a loving family. It all comes down to mindset and discipline. I always focused on eating healthy, exercising, and taking care of myself the best ways that I could.

As someone who repaired elevators for a living, all too often, I would arrive at a job, and the elevator was broken. This meant constantly having to trek up many flights of stairs, with all of my tools and gear, to reach a building's roof. Constant stairclimbing certainly helped keep me in shape. I also went to the gym at 5:00am five days a week. Plus, I had some exercise equipment, like a rowing machine, in my home that I used often.

For me, staying healthy also meant avoiding alcohol. When I was in the Navy, I smoked a bit but later quit at the encouragement of my kids when they were young. Even today, while I can no longer make it to the gym, I have a physical fitness expert come to my home several times a week to help keep my body as functional as possible.

DEVELOPING AND MAINTAINING A STRONG WORK ETHIC

Having strong family values came from my parents and is something I've tried hard to pass down to my children and grandchildren. I was the youngest of three children. My parents and sister have passed on, but my brother Jack just turned 97. He now lives in an assisted living facility near my home, so I see and speak with him regularly. We have remained very close. My father was a licensed electrician by trade. It's from him that I learned how to work with my hands and developed an interest in repairing and restoring things.

At age 13 or 14, I had my first taste of entrepreneurship when I took on a newspaper route. I had about 100 customers. Each customer paid 18 cents per week but often gave me a two-cent tip. I also made 1.5 cents per newspaper, per day for delivering it. This was big money back then.

Having money that I earned myself taught me fiscal responsibility at an early age. It also taught me that working hard paid off, as I was able to afford treats, like a weekly ice cream sundae for myself, because I had my own money.

My father also had a passion for building and rebuilding cars and trucks, and it's something he got me interested in as well at an early age.

When I was 16, I was able to buy my own van, which I then refurbished and maintained myself.

For a few years after the newspaper route, I used the truck to pick up garbage from my neighbors' houses and drop it off at the dump. They'd pay me 25 cents per barrel, so I was able to make a few bucks doing that.

After graduating high school in 1948, I attended Franklin Tech and studied to become an electrician. When I graduated, my father introduced me to someone in the elevator business who gave me a job at age 19. This was in 1950. A year later, I joined the U.S. Navy and served until 1955. I was then in the reserve for four additional years.

One thing I learned from my time in the Navy was how to get along with people. This is a skill that's served me well throughout the rest of my life. After all, more than 360 of us were living and working in very tight quarters aboard the USS Hawkins—a Gearing-class destroyer that was operational during World War II and the Korean War. I made some close friends in the Navy, including the guy who would become my brother-in-law. I introduced him to my sister while we were on leave.

While I traveled to exotic places around the world while in the Navy, I learned that the United States is the best place to live. We have a hell of a country here. These days, I don't think young people realize or appreciate that. It was during this time I married my wife. We dated before I went into the service and then got married while I was on leave in 1953.

I served in the U.S. Navy from 1951 to 1955 aboard the USS Hawkins. After my service, I joined Payne Elevator, where I worked until 1968. In 1969, once our children were in school full-time, my wife, Virginia, and I decided to start our own business. Along with two partners, we founded City Elevator.

One of our business partners had different philosophies about how to grow the business. He wanted to pursue large projects involving installing elevators in newly constructed skyscrapers.

There was a lot of money to be made doing this, but it was also very risky. When an elevator company installs elevators in a new building, it has to lay out the funds for the equipment and labor. However, we don't get paid for the project until the building is completely finished and it is cleared to open its doors. Thus, it could take several years to get paid.

I saw there was a less glamorous but equally profitable route to go, which involved inspecting, maintaining, and repairing existing elevators. My partner also wanted to hire his friends to work in the office, which was not needed at the time. Based on my experience, one formula that worked for my business was that for every three employees we had out in the field doing inspections, maintenance, or repair work, we needed one supervisor in the office to manage them.

If there were too many supervisors in the office, the company would become too top heavy. It was all about finding the right balance that worked from a management and financial standpoint. There are many types of businesses, in many different industries, that need to find and maintain that perfect balance to maintain efficiency while controlling costs.

In 1972, Virginia, John L. McHugh, and I sold our interest in City Elevator and purchased Embree Elevator—the business we operate today. We used the money I made from selling City Elevator and from some real estate I owned to acquire Embree Elevator. My business partner, my wife, and I had great passion and drive. And this time, I made sure we all shared the same philosophies and goals for operating and growing the business.

Luckily, my partner had a friend who was a business consultant. He agreed to give us some advice. It turned out, this guy was one of the entrepreneurs behind the launch and early success of Dunkin' Donuts (which is now a $16.9 billion per year business), so he clearly knew what he was doing. He was very helpful when it came to initially building a strong foundation for what would become Embree Elevator.

We'd have clients sign long-term contracts, so we could more easily predict our income and take on less financial risk. Back then, on days when I would meet with prospective or existing clients, I would need to dress up in a nice business suit.

Then, once the business meetings were done, I'd literally need to find a phone booth or restroom to change into my work clothes, grab my tools, and then get my hands dirty doing the elevator repairs we were hired to do.

Not only did I have to juggle many responsibilities, but I also had to change outfits multiple times each day, based on the meetings I had to attend and the work that needed to get done.

We also found reliable lawyers, insurance agents, and bankers who were very helpful during the early days of Embree Elevator. And since I am a firm believer in networking and mentoring, I often sought out advice from other executives in the elevator industry.

We had regular industry meetings back then. Everyone was willing to share their knowledge and advice freely, whether or not we were competitors. Being able to ask questions and get answers from experts was always very helpful, but it's probably not something that's as readily available to entrepreneurs today.

That said, I definitely recommend attending networking events and industry gatherings or conventions. This is a great way to develop an understanding of what's happening in your industry and meet people who might prove to be very helpful to you in the future.

Of course, there were also many times when I had to make decisions on my own. Part of my business mindset meant being willing to try new things. If something failed, I'd try something different and keep experimenting until I discovered what actually worked.

I tried to avoid taking unnecessary risks, but when I did, they were almost always calculated risks. I did as much research as I could, so I was better able to make intelligent decisions. I found this extra effort often leads to a successful outcome. Being brave enough to try new things in business, but being willing and able to pivot when necessary, is part of what it means to be a good entrepreneur.

You don't need to be working in the elevator industry to understand that life has its ups and downs. For us in this industry, this statement is a bit more literal than for others. Unfortunately, not every decision or action in business works the way you want it to. Learning to handle failure and setbacks is part of being a professional.

You want to learn from your mistakes but never allow failures to break you emotionally or increase your fear. It's all part of the process. Instead of adopting a negative attitude, maintaining a positive one helped keep me motivated. I believe that when something bad happens, it could often be turned into something good over time. And this is often the case.

One important lesson I learned early on is that as a business operator, as much as you might want to, you cannot control everything, or handle everything by yourself. The unexpected sometimes happens, or it becomes necessary to delegate tasks and responsibilities to others. This means making sure you trust the people you work with and understand their strengths and weaknesses.

For example, if I knew that one of my employees might have a personality clash with a client, but was otherwise extremely competent, I'd make sure I sent that person out on different jobs, where I knew they'd be able to succeed and keep the alternate client happy.

In the elevator industry, many employees are union members. As a small business owner, I value working with union labor because union workers are highly trained and experienced, and they bring a strong sense of professionalism and pride to every job. Their skills, safety standards, and reliability make a tremendous difference in the quality of the final product, and I deeply respect the craft and dedication they represent. The one challenge for a company of my size is that I don't have the flexibility to handpick the specific individuals I'd like from the union pool—workers are assigned based on availability. Larger companies often have the scale to benefit more fully from established union systems, while smaller firms like mine sometimes have to adapt to the structure. Still, I appreciate that working with union professionals ensures a consistent level of excellence and helps sustain a strong, skilled workforce for the entire industry.

Again, my ability to build and maintain relationships and stay positive was always a huge asset when dealing with union-related issues that directly impacted my business. Part of my relationship building strategy is to be a good listener. I try to quickly determine what the other person really wants and what their motivations are.

When we first became a union shop, it happened very quickly. At the time, we were charging $10 per hour for labor. The union, however, required us to charge three times that. If I had not already had really strong, long-term personal relationships with our customers, we would have lost most of them once we raised our rates.

For my clients, I tried to increase our rates slowly. Plus, we had long-term contracts that spelled out a rate that could not be suddenly changed. For a while, we took a financial loss since we'd bill out $10 per hour and pay our people $30 per hour. I did this to keep our clients and allow our business to continue operating as smoothly as possible during the transition period.

This was probably the most stressful time I ever experienced as a business operator. I was the owner of my business, but for the first time, I realized I was not fully in charge. This required me to learn new management skills, plus come up with new ways to handle my employees in a manner that meshed with union requirements and policies.

Our success at Embree Elevator became a reality in part because we consistently provided top-notch work. We were also open and honest with our customers. This remains our business strategy today, and it's why we've been able to hold on to some of our clients for several decades. People still come to us for our experience, reliability, and skill, and our reputation.

SOMETIMES, THE BEST BUSINESS STRATEGY IS TO TURN DOWN NEW BUSINESS

Over the years, we've had potential customers who have wanted to hire us, but I've turned down the new business. You may be thinking, who in their right mind would turn down business? Well, it often came down to whether we could do the job properly, in a way that the customer would want and could afford. If they found us through the Yellow Pages, I'd always ask what happened to their previous elevator maintenance and repair company.

If I discovered that the previous company used inferior parts or installed the wrong type of equipment based on the client's actual needs, I would often refrain from trying to fix what could become a very expensive mess. Plus, there were potential clients who had a reputation for not paying their bills on time. Those too need to be avoided.

Since I was able to call competitors and discuss clients with them, if a potential customer came to us out of the blue, I'd often call the elevator company they previously worked with to discover what went wrong from their point of view. As a result, I had the potential client and their former elevator company's perspectives to consider before taking on the potential new job. Again, the more information I could gather, the more educated decisions I could make.

A lot also came down to resources and manpower, and how to best utilize what we had available. If a new job would stretch our resources too thin, and the profit potential was not necessarily there, I'd turn down the work but refer the potential customer to a competitor.

For example, Embree Elevator has always worked within a specific geographic area. If a potential customer approached us from outside that area, I'd need to consider the commuting costs, and the extra billable hours it would take to handle that client's needs.

AS AN ENTREPRENEUR, KEEP AN OPEN MIND

Especially in the 1950s and 1960s, it was common practice for business owners to stick with hiring people from specific ethnic or religious backgrounds, and to rarely hire women, except to handle secretarial work. This was never what I believed.

When it came to hiring employees, I focused on their experience and skills. I considered what they could contribute to my business, and what sort of work ethic they had. I always tried to avoid people who would show up for work a few minutes late on a regular basis, and then never consider working past 5:00pm, when the workday was supposed to come to an end.

I also had an open mind about the contribution women could make in business. After all, I invited my wife to be a business partner. She also handled the company's payroll and some of the bookkeeping, in addition to doing some secretarial work from the office and from home (while also raising our kids). Later, when it came time to pass the business along to the next generation, instead of one of my sons, it was my daughter Carol whom I chose to take over.

Her husband wound up joining the business later. He was an accountant, but also very comfortable around computers. He became a driving force when it came to keeping the computer technology we used in the office and in the field up to date.

Carol started her professional career as a registered nurse. When she wanted to start a family, she was still on an overnight shift and worried that the hours might make childcare difficult. My wife had been able to do much of the bookkeeping and other job responsibilities from home so when my wife decided to retire and give the job to Carol, it allowed a flexible work-from-home position. She decided to leave nursing and join the family business. She has always been a good communicator, but to this day, she's stricter than I ever was as a boss.

When it comes to the workplace, I am someone who believes everyone should be treated equally and fairly. Over the years, I have proven myself to be honest and loyal toward my employees, and I expect the same from them. I think it's this understanding that has allowed me to hang on to a handful of my employees for 40 or more years, and then have their children come work for my business.

Throughout the decades I managed Embree Elevator, I tried to think of my employees as my buddies. We often went out for lunch together. However, at the end of the day, they went home (or to the bar), and I went home to my family. We never socialized during our off hours or on weekends. This was also true with my former partners (excluding my wife and children, of course).

I am also someone who believes in helping my employees. If a health issue arose, for example, I was first in line to help them find the medical assistance and support they needed. And if there was a family emergency, I had no trouble giving an employee the time off they required to deal with the situation.

There was one employee years ago who got injured on the job and could no longer repair elevators. Instead of letting him go, I brought him into the office. He would answer phones and deal with client calls. He did a great job, because he knew all about elevators and how to interact with the clients to address their needs.

Also, as some of our elevator technicians got too old to work in the field doing repairs, we'd help them transition to become elevator inspectors. This allowed them to put their knowledge and experience to work without having to do the physical labor. I always took it upon myself to look out for the long-term well-being of my employees any way I could.

Of course, I took everything on a case-by-case basis. While trying to be fair, I had to avoid being taken advantage of by lazy employees, or those who do not showcase a professional work ethic. Another reason to care for your employees is because you never know which competitors will try to poach them from you.

I've seen people quit their job and jump ship to another company over a 25-cent-per hour salary increase. An important part about being an employer is learning ways to keep your employees happy, interested, and loyal. Sometimes, offering a good work environment is more important to an employee than a slight pay raise they might get working for a competitor.

It's also helpful when your trusted employees know people in the industry who are looking for a new job. I believe it's often easier to hire someone based on a recommendation and referral than it is to take on the risk of hiring someone who comes to you on their own. Positive word of mouth has always been—and continues to be—a powerful way to find new employees and land new customers.

2

When It Comes to Life and Business, It's Much Better with Family

"If you can laugh together, you can work together."

ROBERT ORBEN

IN THE previous chapter, I touched on how important family is, and how mine has always been a tremendous support system in my personal and professional life. I believe family members should always be there to support each other and live by a "family first" motto. Having that support system allows people, including myself, to achieve things we could never do on our own.

I found that as people grow up and their responsibilities change, the type of support they need from family also evolves. This is usually a gradual change, so it's not always noticeable, but as each family member enters into a new stage in their personal or professional life, the type and level of support they need changes. This is more apparent when you're raising kids.

Over the years, I've learned you can't force your support on someone else. You can, however, be there as a role model and teach by example. You can walk the walk, not just talk the talk. I had a loving relationship with my wife, and we shared a mutual respect for each other. We went to church on Sundays, I did not drink, and I gave up smoking when my kids were young.

My children also saw me working hard and experienced me being there to spend quality time with them. In fact, while my wife prepared dinner for the family during the week, I prepared dinner almost every Sunday. Our kids noticed all this as they grew up.

Beyond letting people see you as a role model, you can let them know you are there when you're needed. This includes being there to provide emotional or financial support, advice, or anything else. Being a supportive partner or parent is very different from trying to control someone else's life or insisting that your way of doing things is the best and only way.

My own need for support has also changed dramatically over time. For much of my adult life, I provided a strong support system for my children, while my wife and I supported each other. Now, as I've gotten much older, the roles and responsibilities have changed somewhat. My wife is no longer with us. My now adult children and grandchildren (all of whom are now adults) play an important role in my day-to-day care—and have done so without being asked.

In my extended family, we all help and support each other. I believe this is a key reason why those of us who are or have been married have remained happy together for so long. My parents were together for 75 years, and my marriage lasted for more than 66 years, until my wife passed away. And those of my children who are married have each been with their partners for more than 30 years, and their relationships are still going strong.

I should also mention that my grandparents, parents, in-laws, siblings, and now some of my children have always lived in fairly close proximity within Bedford, Massachusetts. For decades, Carol and her husband have lived in a house next to mine. As a result, I've had the pleasure of spending a lot of quality time with them outside of work, and with their children (my grandchildren) as they were growing up.

Due to our family-wide support system, we've all been able to achieve success in whatever it is we've set out to do on a personal or professional level. These days, I don't think too many parents realize just how important it is to really be there to support their children, and how much of an impact that support can have on their entire lives.

Couples wholeheartedly supporting each other is also a key for a successful marriage. After growing up with two supportive parents, this was automatically something I tried to replicate and then pass down to my children.

I think being around so much support while growing up and during my adulthood, I've come to care about the well-being of other people, too. This includes my employees. This attitude towards others is one of the things that has set me apart from many other business operators.

Most business operators tend to care much more about their own success and take their employee's hard work for granted. By showing support for my employees over the decades, they've been very loyal. I also think they work harder and work better with each other as a team, knowing their boss is looking out for them and their best interests.

When you blur the line between your home life and work life by inviting family members to be part of a business, the family dynamic changes. Embree Elevator is a multi-generational family business, and beyond those relatives who have worked for the business over the years, it's been able to financially support members of the extended family when they've needed it.

There have been many TV series and movies about the back-stabbing and the quest for money and control that occurs between family members who are working for a family business. At least when it comes to my family, that's not been our reality. Those Hollywood depictions are absolutely nothing like what it's been like working with my loved ones.

ACHIEVING A WORK/LIFE BALANCE

This chapter is all about the importance of family, and how to successfully achieve a work/life balance. Yes, this can be accomplished, even if you're an entrepreneur running a successful business. However, you need to understand that having a work/life balance is something you need to achieve with proper planning, time management, and discipline.

A successful work/life balance does not just happen by itself—especially when there are so many work-related distractions and responsibilities that can so easily keep you away from your family and from being able to find time for yourself.

During the decades I was running Embree Elevators, my goal was to get home each day in time for dinner and also be able to spend all day on Sundays with my family. In addition, I made time for myself every morning at 5:00am to work out at the gym.

So, to achieve my work/life balance, before taking into account work-related emergencies and issues that required my attention after hours, on weekends, and on holidays, a typical day for me began around 4:30am and ended at around 9:00pm.

As the Boss, I Tried to Understand Everyone's Workload

I believe one of the other reasons why my company was successful is because as the boss, I liked being in the office and spending time in the field and actually getting my hands dirty doing repair and maintenance work.

I had first-hand experience working in all aspects of the business, instead of just sitting behind a desk and delegating work to everyone else. I believe my employees and the family members who work for the company noticed and respected my hands-on approach.

These days, many busy people talk about trying to achieve a successful work/life balance, but it's all talk. Some people opt to put more focus on their career and quest for more money, while others put emphasis on their family, and allow their job or career to suffer.

To me, a good work/life balance means being able to meet all of your work-related obligations, but also find the time to spend with family, enjoy personal time, and have a well-rounded life outside of work.

Achieving a true work/life balance is very difficult, especially today. It requires a tremendous amount of planning. You also need top-notch organizational and time management skills, and the drive to establish and maintain a balance in your life. Sure, compromises will need to be made based on situations that arise, but these are things you need to have a plan to deal with, so they cause as little disruption in your work/life balance as possible.

For someone who works at a company and has a traditional 9:00am to 5:00pm, Monday through Friday job, creating and maintaining a work/life balance is a lot easier. If you don't have a fixed work schedule or have responsibilities that vary from day to day because you're running your own business, it becomes much harder to find time for everything.

One way I set the tone for my work/life balance was to faithfully visit the gym every morning at 5:00am. Not only was this a healthy thing to do, but it also gave me time to focus on myself and clear my head as I prepared for the day ahead.

My goal was to work from 8:00am to 6:00pm, six days a week. And when I left work, my focus was on my family and personal life. Since most everyone else at work showed up at 9:00am, and then ended their work day at 5:00pm, this gave me time every morning and evening to plan and do what I needed to do at work with far fewer distractions.

Regardless of what was happening at the office, when 6:00pm rolled around, I was hungry and tired, so anything that wasn't done (unless it was an emergency) got put off until the next business day. This is where personal discipline was important. I knew what needed to get done and when, set my priorities, and forced myself to go home instead of trying to do a bunch of last-minute tasks at the end of the day that could have kept me at work another two or three hours.

This was a strategy I needed to teach Carol when she started working for the company. She shares the same work ethic as me. At the end of the day, she'd want to stay late and keep working until we literally had to turn off the lights on her. As a business leader, you must have a strong work ethic, but it's equally important to force yourself to maintain a work/life balance and stay disciplined when it comes to leaving work each day.

During the years when I was both in the office and working in the field as the business owner, if an emergency job came in during the night and I needed to wake up and deal with it, this was always in addition to my regular work schedule. When this occurred, I'd deal with the emergency and then go into the office to start my regular work day. If the field job wasn't complete, I'd either stay to finish it, or have someone come in and replace me to finish it, so I could be in the office. It all depended on where I was needed the most that day.

When there was no emergency to deal with, I focused on maintaining my 8:00am to 6:00pm schedule. In the early days, I'd work either a full day or half-day on Saturdays, too. Later on, once the company was more established, this was not always necessary, so I was able to spend Saturdays and Sundays at home with my family.

Without a doubt, being able to maintain that regular workday schedule as much as possible had a positive impact on my family relationships. When the kids were young, I knew that my wife was taking really good care of them, because she would typically work part-time from home at that point. She would call me at work if there was an issue. This gave me peace of mind when it came to the wellbeing of my family on a day-to-day basis.

My wife understood that I needed to work long hours and fully supported me. We both appreciated the perks of owning and running a business. That made things much easier for both of us. And in regard to our kids, they saw us working hard and learned by example that having a strong work ethic is important for success in life.

From the time my kids were young, I explained that I worked so hard for their benefit and to provide them with a comfortable life. It helped them understand why I was not always home. I never wanted them to mistakenly believe I worked hard to avoid being with them.

Once they understood this, it made things easier on everyone. Of course, I made a point to be there for all the milestone events in my children's and grandchildren's lives. Those always took priority.

For me, maintaining a good work/life balance was one of the biggest ongoing challenges I faced as a business owner. However, because I became good at it, I experienced some great rewards. Over the years, experiencing a work/life balance kept me motivated and energized, and helped me to properly deal with all of life's stresses.

In my opinion, part of maintaining a work/life balance is being able to decide what constitutes a good reason to work extra hours and what does not. This also applies to personal responsibilities. If a family issue arose, it was necessary to determine if it was something my wife could handle until I got home, or if I needed to leave work early on that day to deal with a situation with the kids, for example. Because my wife and I worked so well as life partners, she was instrumental in helping me make the right decision whenever something came up.

As the business owner, I understand that no employee will ever have quite the same level of dedication or motivation as I do—and I don't expect them to. This company is my livelihood, my investment, and something I've built with my own hands. I fully recognize that for most people, a job is a job, not a calling. But what I do expect, and what every good employee should bring, is integrity and pride in their work. That means showing up ready to work—not just prepared to clock in.

What frustrates me most are the "clock-watchers." They arrive at 9:00 a.m. but spend the first 20 minutes making coffee, chatting, and easing into the day. By 11:30, their focus shifts to where they'll go for lunch, and somehow their one-hour lunch turns into 90 minutes once you factor in travel time. Then, by 4:30, they're wrapping up early, changing shoes, and chatting by the door, waiting for 5:00 to hit. On paper, they've put in eight hours. In reality, it's closer to six and a half.

This kind of behavior doesn't just hurt productivity—it sends the wrong message to everyone else. When one person treats the job like a timecard game, others start to think it's acceptable. Before long, that attitude spreads, and the standard for what's "normal" begins to slip. I expect fairness, accountability, and respect—for the job, for their coworkers, and for the effort we're all putting in to keep this business strong.

Even before my daughter and my son-in-law took over the day-to-day operation of the business, I started to step back slowly, so over the past ten years or so, I have had a much lighter schedule and far fewer work responsibilities. As a result, I have been able to spend much more time with my wife (until she passed away), children, and grandchildren. This extra time spent with them has meant so much to me and made all of the hard work throughout my life well worth it.

TREAT FAMILY MEMBERS AND EMPLOYEES THE SAME AT WORK

As the boss, when I see someone continuously exhibiting a "clock watcher" mentality or not fully meeting their job responsibilities on a regular basis,

I take this into consideration when it comes time to award promotions or pay raises.

For a business that doesn't operate under union guidelines, if an employee is consistently not meeting expectations, they can easily be fired. But as a union shop, as the boss, I often had to give them second and third chances before I could let them go.

Another common issue running a family business is determining everyone's salary. Relatives tend to expect to be paid more than they're worth, simply because they're part of the family.

My policy has always been you get paid based on the position you hold and the responsibilities you take on—the same guidelines I used for all of my employees. Relatives got no preferential treatment, automatic raises, or guaranteed promotions.

Anyone who doesn't appreciate the salary they're being paid (which is always a fair wage) is free to work elsewhere. I am all about fairness for everyone when it comes to salaries and job titles. Being a relative does not get you preferential treatment.

If someone wanted a raise or promotion, whether you're a relative or not, I always spelled out exactly what was expected of them. Only if someone lived up to their job responsibilities did they become eligible for the raise or promotion.

These days, it's common for employers to create a detailed employee handbook and provide (in writing) an in-depth job description to each employee. Looking back, this would have been a good strategy for me to implement. I always covered this information through in-person discussions. My daughter now has her own policy.

Nobody gets special treatment. I think this has allowed us to avoid a lot of family conflict when it comes to finances. I always wanted my relatives to be happy working for me. If they were not content with how they were treated, or with the salary they were paid, I did not want them going around to the other employees saying what a jerk their father or uncle is.

I'd prefer they go off and do their own thing when someone is not happy working for my business. If things were not working out with a relative, there have been times when I have asked them to leave the company. I was not doing this to be mean. The decision was made for the best interest of the business and all of the employees. Ultimately, it's my business, and I needed to make the difficult decisions that impacted everyone involved with it.

I also made sure my employees, including my relatives, knew I would be checking up on them. I would often go into the field and visit employees on the job site, and at the same time meet with the clients in person. I would ask the clients how we're doing, and about the quality of service we're providing. I did this to make sure the clients and our employees were always satisfied.

In other words, it was clear that I was always accessible to my employees and paying attention to the quality of their work. I was also readily available to our clients, who could express any concerns they had directly with me. I tried to always keep the lines of communication open.

Not only did my employees in the field need to meet or exceed my expectations, but they also needed for the customers to remain happy. Supervision is an important aspect of being a good manager and a strong business leader.

One lesson I learned early on was that paying relatives a lot more than they're worth to the company does not make fiscal sense for the long-term prosperity of the business. If the business can't stay profitable, it impacts the whole family, all employees, and their respective families. It was always my job to focus on the big picture.

I really encouraged my kids and grandchildren to attend college, so they'd learn what other opportunities are out there in the world beyond what Embree Elevator or living in Bedford, Massachusetts could offer them. Once they knew their options, they could decide for themselves whether working for the family business was best for them.

THE PROS AND CONS OF RUNNING A FAMILY BUSINESS WITH CLOSE RELATIVES

It was ultimately my responsibility to make sure the business always continued to be solvent, since so many family members were relying on the company's success. For this reason, I took risk taking and spending the company's money a lot more seriously than I might have done otherwise. I'll focus more on risk taking in the next chapter.

One benefit that having a family business offered is that all of my kids and grandchildren had the security of knowing that they could pursue whatever career they wanted, but they would never be out of work. Any of them were welcome to join the family business at any time.

Throughout the years, several of my kids and later my grandchildren would come to work for us. Some stayed, while others ultimately went on to pursue their own professional interests, but always knew Embree Elevator was there if they wanted or needed to come back.

I hope the knowledge that they always had a place to work if they needed it provided them with a sense of security, which is something that most people who didn't have a successful family business to rely on would have.

When my kids were growing up, if I needed to go on a night call or an emergency call on weekends to fix an elevator, I'd sometimes take one of my kids with me to show them what the business was all about. Then, when they got older, if they wanted to join the business, I'd start them at the bottom, so to speak. This allowed them to slowly learn all aspects of the business.

Carol, who now runs the day-to-day operations of the business, started out answering the phones. She never became a mechanic or electrician, but she finished college. At first, she pursued a career as a nurse, but when she left that to join Embree Elevator, she learned all about the operation and management of the business. This allowed her to eventually step in to run it. This was a position she earned after demonstrating her abilities.

WAYS TO OVERCOME WORK-RELATED FAMILY DISAGREEMENTS

When multiple family members are involved in the same business, disagreements will arise. This is to be expected, whether the issues have to do with finances, operational changes, or how the company will grow. This is on top of the typical disagreements and personal conflicts that family members might experience that have nothing to do with a business.

As the business owner, I quickly learned that running a company takes far more than just skill in the trade—it's about balancing people, deadlines, and details from every direction. Between managing the office, coordinating with vendors, keeping customers satisfied, and overseeing the laborers on site, there's never really an "off" switch. My sons saw that firsthand as they grew up around the business. They saw the early mornings, the late nights, and the constant problem-solving that comes with ownership.

After they graduated from college, when the time came for them to choose their own paths, they decided to join the union and work as trained laborers rather than step into the office or management side. I respected that completely. They had seen the pressure and responsibility that come with running a company and wanted to focus on perfecting their craft—to build, to create, and to be part of the tangible results of the work we do. That's an honorable choice, and I take pride in the fact that they wanted to stay connected to the same line of work, just from a different perspective.

Because they shared my last name, there was always a perception that they might receive special treatment. To avoid that, and to earn respect on their own merits, they chose to work for other companies. I admire that decision. It showed integrity and self-respect—the same qualities that make any good tradesperson or businessperson successful. In the end, they're carving their own paths, just as I did, and contributing to the same industry in their own way. I couldn't be prouder of that.

Of course, when a disagreement happens at work with a family member, it tends to seep into our personal lives. That's when things get extra difficult. This is why having good communication and conflict management skills are useful as the boss. Keeping an open line of communication, listening, being able to make compromises, and being creative when finding solutions has proved very helpful to me over the years.

I think the biggest benefit of having relatives work in a family business is you get to spend more time with everyone. This can help build a closer-knit family dynamic. It's not always easy, however.

HOW I PASS MY ENTREPRENEURIAL SPIRIT AND WORK ETHIC TO THE NEXT GENERATION

Thus far, I've described some of the ways my wife and I worked hard to create a close-knit family, and then pass down some of our wisdom, work ethic, and family values to our children and their children.

Based on how my now-adult children turned out, I am proud to say that my wife and I seemed to have done a really good job helping them to grow up into responsible, honest, hardworking, loyal, and successful adults.

Don't just take my word for it, however. Just as I am openly sharing my life's ups and downs, accomplishments and failures, and advice with you, I asked my son-in-law Cliff to reflect on the impact I've had on his life and the ongoing success of Embree Elevator now that he and my daughter have taken the reins.

I put together a list of questions and then asked my son-in-law to provide answers openly and honestly, with the goal of sharing with you (the reader) the business and life-related wisdom he learned from me and from being part of the family business.

The interview you're about to read is in no way edited by me, nor did I try to persuade my son-in-law to answer any of these questions in a specific way. From this interview, you will discover what it's like, in today's business world, to run a family business hand-in-hand with your spouse. Here's what he chose to share.

Meet My Son-In-Law Cliff Washer, Chief Financial Officer of Embree Elevator

How would you describe me, and what qualities do you think helped me become successful?
Jim is the kind of person who enters a room full of unfamiliar people and feels right at home. He mixes into groups with an endless library of light-hearted jokes that 95 percent of us could never remember.

When you first met Carol, did you think she'd ultimately be joining the family business?
Carol and I met as freshmen while attending Northeastern University. She was a nursing student, and I was a criminal justice student. The furthest thing from our minds was getting involved in any business. My goal was to become a Massachusetts State Trooper. Her plan was to become a registered nurse.

As we became more serious, I lost interest in criminal justice for a handful of reasons, which led me to transfer to the business school. Throughout our time in college, we never discussed anything other than her nursing career, and my accounting/finance career.

When you got married, were there ever any plans for you two to work together?
No. Carol was working as an RN in the stepdown unit at Lahey Clinic. She developed a specialization in cardiology. This experience would later prove to be invaluable as Jim and Ginny aged and began to experience profound medical issues. She loved the complexity of cardiology and was a natural at it. Nearly 40 years after changing careers, she is still brilliant with medical issues of all kinds.

At what point did you decide to leave your previous accounting work and join Embree Elevator?
When Carol joined the company, we began having lengthy discussions,

as couples often do, about what she was doing. The accounting systems at the company were what I call 'old style.' They worked fine for the time, but during our discussions, we wanted to update the systems using more modern technologies.

My work as a Certified Public Accountant provided me with knowledge about technology that could help the company's processes work more efficiently. The first Embree computer was set up in our kitchen. It was a 100MB machine the salesman said we would never fill up.

We had asked Jim what he thought about moving onto a computer, and he was happy to let us move forward to modernize the company's accounting processes. His love of the business has always been with elevator work, and specifically the personal relationships he developed—with staff, clients, inspectors, and anyone else he encountered.

Back-of-the-house management was never an area he particularly enjoyed. It was during this time I became more closely connected with the company. I started to see an opportunity to lend some of what I had learned toward helping the company grow.

When did you join the company, and what were the circumstances surrounding this decision?

I joined the company back in July 1994. Carol and I had been discussing approaching Jim with the idea for quite some time. Family circumstances made any moves of that type very complicated until the summer/fall of 1993.

When it seemed the time was right to discuss possibilities with Jim, I needed to find an opportunity and the guts to start the discussion. In mid-November 1993, Jim had replaced the clad boards on the front of his house. It was about 40 degrees, and we both had one-piece snow suits on. We were trying to stay warm from the New England cold winds.

It's a long story, but here's the short version. While we were sitting on scaffolding and painting the house, I finally summoned the courage to tell Jim that I thought there were some ways I could help the company grow. I asked if he would be okay with me writing up a five year business plan encompassing where I thought we could take the business.

Jim being Jim he said, 'Sure, put it together and I'll take a look.' It took a little while to complete, but by July 1994, I was in place and ready to go.

What got you interested in the elevator industry?

I became interested in the industry through having a father-in-law who eats, sleeps, and breathes elevators. Conversations would regularly lead back around to elevators. When out driving in the Boston area, for example, he was constantly pointing out buildings he had worked in, and explained what type of elevator was there. He would also nearly always know the name and family history of the owner or manager of each building.

I discovered the elevator industry is a unique animal in the realm of service businesses. The work is among the most dangerous, short of crane operators and Alaskan lobstermen. Elevator systems in use today range from brand new to 75 years old, but some are even older.

Many of the elevator companies from the past have been gobbled up by larger entities. Simultaneously, new companies have formed and have in turn been acquired as well. To be with a company that has the history of Embree Elevator is both an honor and a great responsibility.

Jim has always been open to new ideas. He has only rarely stepped up and said, 'Hold on, wait a second there,' when new ideas were presented. He has a keen eye for movements that might place the company at risk.

When you joined the company, what was your job title and key responsibilities?

I joined Embree as a CPA back in 1994, with the title of Controller.

That title was later changed to Chief Financial Officer. My main responsibilities were everything related to finance, accounting, and strategic planning.

On a day-to-day basis, Carol handled all billings and collections. In a small business, defined functional responsibilities are often hard to nail down. On Monday, I might be meeting with the bank to work on maintaining the company's working capital line of credit, and Tuesday I could find myself on a forklift assisting with unloading a large shipment of materials.

One of the most rewarding aspects of managing an operation of this size is the exposure I get on a daily basis to every possible facet of running the business.

How and where did you gain the interest and knowledge about computers and technology?

Throughout my career I have been obsessed with always moving forward with the available new technology. Jim has been very patient with me as we moved onto new more advanced accounting platforms set up to help us more accurately manage overall and project costs. Additionally, Carol has a skill for system implementation none of us realized.

Tapping into that skill has been critical to the successful launch of our current system, which has now been in place, with numerous upgrades, since 2003. As of today, we are able to oversee financial operations with detailed analysis in a way we could have only wished for in the past. This enables us to spot negative trends more rapidly and make the necessary adjustments to head off potential problems.

What regrets, if any, have you had about joining the family business?

I would not say 'regrets,' but I would say there have been 'complexities.' Family businesses are a minefield of potential issues. Many have shown themselves, but with patience, and sometimes a thick skin, we have been able to work through them and keep moving forward.

I think family businesses can be problematic if you are a reactionary person. Staying calm and being slow to anger will serve you well and help to prevent your emotions from taking actions before your brain has had a chance to think everything through.

Early on, did you have any issues taking direction from me or your wife?

I remember my first week, I moved a trash can in the office to be next to my desk. Jim walked by and tossed a balled up piece of paper where the trash can used to be. He looked around and found the can where I moved it.

He said, "25 years in that spot over there, I guess it's better over here." That may not seem like much, because he said it with a chuckle. However, it signaled to me that slow changes might be better moving forward.

I learned I should not just move things around or upset the apple cart too quickly. However, I don't recall any serious altercations. Typically, if I thought an idea was a bit edgy, or it had a little more than normal risk, Carol and I would work it through and beat it up until we thought we had a good grip on what might happen. Then, Carol would discuss it with Jim on the side to gauge his reaction and get feedback we could use to streamline or kill that idea.

At one point, we had an active debate about whether to change the company name to Embree Elevator or Embree & White Elevator. There were convincing arguments in both directions. We were at an impasse and staring across the conference room table at each other. Then, out of nowhere, Jim pulled out a coin and said, "Call it in the air." I replied, "Jim, you can't make a decision this important like th..... Heads!"

The coin came down heads. We then became known as Embree Elevator. We would have done as well either way, but it has always been my favorite example of Jim finding a way to calm things down and to keep us moving forward. A good CEO, like Jim, knows when to step in and keep the troops from tearing things up.

How did you go about learning the elevator industry and how Embree Elevator operated as a business?

My initial education came from just being a fly on the wall as Jim and Carol spoke about the business. They often discussed business-related issues while I was in the room. Jim's love of the business meant he spoke about it often. Picking up how the industry operates started for me when Carol and I first got married in 1985.

What changes did you want to make upon joining the business? Did you get any pushback from me or Carol?

I would not call it pushback. I wanted the business to grow, and we did that. The road to get there was not a straight one, however. In small business management, you have to be flexible, and able to move with the tides.

Jim's theory, which I agree with, was that slow growth is best. With fast growth comes increased risk. Jim has always said if growing means working more and making less, he'd rather work less and make more. You may have to think about that a bit, but it makes great sense.

How does the dynamic between you and Carol change between when you're at the office and when you're at home?

Home may sometimes feel like an extension of work. I could say that we separate work life from home life, just like you often hear people say in television interviews. That would not be accurate. I believe those people are not being fully honest.

We do often make time to get away, and we don't talk about work all the time. But issues with the business don't just freeze at 4:00pm and hold until the next day. We care deeply about this business achieving success, and we are both a bit obsessive. So, discussions at home frequently involve work-related issues that are sticking in our minds.

Is it difficult spending so much time with your spouse at work and at home?
It can be complicated, but we have found ways to manage. One advantage is that we defend each other vociferously with other staff when issues arise. Having a person in the workplace who always has your back is invaluable.

Additionally, if one of us is chasing a rabbit down a hole unnecessarily, we can discuss it at home when things are calm and quiet. That dynamic would be different if your spouse was not aware of the environment surrounding the issue at hand.

What would you say are the secrets to your happy and strong marriage?
I think my wife is gorgeous inside and out. We have been together since 1980, and we drive each other crazy at times. At the end of the day, however, we are a winning team, and we stick together.

The secret to a long, happy, and strong marriage is patience. We all have good and bad days. If you're going to frolic in the good days, you have to support each other in the bad days, too. If you keep that in mind, you can get through anything. Lord knows we have been through hell, and I have never considered anything but supporting Carol.

When a personal or work conflict between you two comes up, how do you resolve it in a way that does not impact your work lives or personal lives?
Disputes are inevitable. If you are confident in your position, but cannot get agreement, then agree to wait and see what develops. If your thoughts are in the right direction, time will prove it out. Focus on the long-term success of the team, not on winning the argument.

Long-term success is the goal, so you always need to keep your eye on the ball.

What were some of the biggest challenges you first faced when joining an established and already successful family business? And has there ever been pushback from employees?

Pushback was inevitable. When you want to change the direction of an entrenched staff, you need to deal with pushback from all angles. Patience and learning are critical.

When I started at Embree, I wanted to make sweeping changes in the machine shop operation. I soon found out the machinist had Jim's ear more than I did as it related to changes. I did not give up. Instead, I backed up and considered a path for success, presented it to Jim, and moved more strategically and slowly. I needed to turn the ship at a pace where shop staff did not realize change was occurring.

Success is measured in a number of ways. Jim was happy with the company's position prior 1994. It was Carol and I who had the vision of a larger operation. Jim was willing to participate, as long as we did not mess up the base of the operation. Managing customer relationships was always priority one for Jim. If we could build the business while maintaining existing relationships he was all in.

What specific career or life lessons have you learned from me that have impacted your life thus far?

Number one for me is Jim's mantra, 'work less, make more' which means, increase revenue through smarter, more efficient operations. At its base, it sounds simplistic. In practice, it is the base of operational strategy that leads to success. When I pushed the company into new installation contracts, we were working far harder but making less money.

Who gains with that? In fact, we were so deep into low margin work, we nearly destroyed the company. Ultimately, we were able to extricate ourselves from this mousetrap and move in a different direction. Jim was patient and let me learn that lesson the hard way.

Thankfully, we escaped, and returned to the 'work less, make more' strategy. With this direction, you focus on taking care of good customers, avoiding bad ones, and setting competitive pricing that leaves you profitable without stretching your neck out to deal with low margin work. We let the competition choke on that type of work.

Jim has a view on life that is enviable. He always looks on the positive side and always has a joke to share. He has old-fashioned silent strength that is always present and not appreciated until it is missing. When times get tough, and stress is at its maximum, Jim will throw in a joke that will break the silence and bring everyone back to the room.

What advice do you have for readers who might be starting a business, or taking over a business with their spouse or significant other?

A calm, patient presence is key. When everyone around you is panicking, no matter how bad the financial picture is, you need to remain calm. Make sure everyone knows you are in it for the long haul and then keep pushing forward.

We have been through the toughest times, payroll was in question, bills were unpaid, and collectors were calling. Throughout that, Carol and I would stare at the ceiling late at night and run through options. We'd ask ourselves, 'What if we did this?' or 'What if we moved that?' until we found a plan that would give us another day, another week, or another month. It is never easy, but it has definitely been worth the struggle.

One lesson I have learned is that the rewards for success are not just financial.

How is working for your family business different from working for another employer?

You are the hub of a wheel that has many family members relying on your success. As the hub, you cannot be fired unexpectedly, but job security depends on your ability to achieve success. You have knowledge and impact on all facets of the business. Failure is not an option.

What have been the biggest obstacles running a business together with your wife and raising children at the same time?
The only obstacle I can think of is that you never leave work completely. There was a point where service calls on weekends were coming to my phone for screening, and I needed to dispatch technicians.

I would sometimes be coaching one of my kids' soccer games on Saturday when my phone would ring and a client required a tech immediately. My assistant coaches knew I was screening calls for work and would have to jump in to assist. This is an example of why you need to surround yourself with good people who are reliable and who have your back.

What life lessons have you learned from me that you've tried to pass down to your children?
I'm not certain of specifics, but as we have lived directly adjacent to our in-laws for 40 years, there is no doubt that Jim's calm demeanor and easy laugh have had an indelible impact on our children.

Is there any other advice you can share with this book's readers about how to succeed working in a family business and maintaining a work/life balance?
Running a family business is a little like running through a minefield wearing cement shoes. Careful navigation is critical. Remain patient, and don't be quick to anger. Be flexible in your thinking. If you are hard headed, you may find fewer people willing to follow. Those people might even rejoice when you fail. Recognize that everyone has strengths and weaknesses. Use those to help manage your business.

How would you describe the legacy that I will eventually leave behind?
Jim has a kind heart, is patient, and loves a good joke. I have never met anyone who did not love him and ask where he was if he was not present. He has a charisma not shared by many. People gravitate toward his presence. You don't learn that. You are born with it. He has touched many and will be missed deeply when he gets called home.

3

Business Success Requires Taking Calculated Risks

"Only those who will risk going too far can possibly find out how far one can go."

T. S. ELIOT

YOU WILL be faced with many uncertainties, regardless of the type of business you're operating and what industry you work in. Fear of the unknown can be very scary. Without taking risks, you can hamper your company's ability to grow or succeed. Taking too many risks or making careless decisions can, however, lead to financial or other pitfalls that could be very hard to recover from.

As an entrepreneur, some risks you'll take will be minor. Whether or not things work out in your favor won't have serious consequences on the long-term success of your business. In these cases, when things do not go as planned, you can chalk them up as a learning experience, do better next time, and try something different in the future.

Taking an acceptable risk or calculated risk is often easier because it means relying on information, facts, statistics, current data, experience, or knowledge to help you make a more educated decision. This can greatly reduce the chances of a negative outcome. Making a business decision based on a calculated risk means you're hopefully dealing with a lower probability of a negative income.

For me, taking a calculated risk is more fun, because the chances of a positive outcome are better. And taking a small, calculated risk would often have little to no negative impact on the business as a whole.

Some risks, especially those that involve large amounts of money, or a potential negative outcome that could be detrimental to your business, can be a lot harder to deal with. When you take any type of risk, there's a chance something negative could happen. You're typically dealing with uncertainties and often forces that are outside of your control.

TYPES OF RISKS YOU'LL LIKELY HAVE TO MANAGE

When approached correctly, with almost any risk in business, there can be a generous reward. There are four main types of risk—*strategic, operational, financial,* and *compliance* related.

A strategic risk relates to the long-term goals or objectives of your business, and whether you'll be able to achieve them by taking a specific action, or by making an important decision that could have positive or negative consequences. Customer demand, sudden changes in the economy, or the actions of a competitor could force the need to take strategic risks.

Operational risks relate to the procedures your company follows to accomplish something specific. This can relate to people, system implementation, or internal processes. Meanwhile financial risk relates to all things having to do with money, including investments, loans/financing, expenditures, income, or actions that could lead to financial growth or loss.

Finally, compliance risk has to do with following laws and regulations or creating internal policies that if not followed could lead to financial penalties, legal issues, or a lack of safety.

When it comes to risk taking or making a decision that involves risk, you're basically playing with probabilities. Based on your decisions or actions, you're hoping for a positive outcome, but there's some uncertainty about what will happen.

Other common types of risks you may encounter as a business operator relate to reputation, security, legal issues, technology, contracts, environmental, and human actions, although there are countless other risk types that may come up as well.

THE PROS AND CONS OF RISK TAKING

Knowing that taking risks is an important part of being a business leader and entrepreneur, learning risk management skills can be extremely beneficial. If you ultimately take on too much risk, make poor or uneducated decisions related to risk, or you do not properly consider the ramifications of risk taking, this could lead to devastating failure and tremendous financial losses.

There are many ways to approach risk taking in business. I have always trusted my gut, although early in my career, I know I sometimes took unnecessary risks or could have done a better job evaluating risks before taking them. That said, whenever I had to take a risk, I did my absolute best to first transform it into a calculated risk.

In technical terms, a calculated risk means you make a decision by weighing the probability of a potential gain versus the potential loss after making careful assessments of the chances of success versus the consequences of failure. The goal is to do what's necessary to lower the chance of failure by making intelligent and well-informed decisions.

To make an informed decision, this might mean doing extensive research, crunching numbers, seeking out advice from others, analyzing trends, reviewing data that's at your disposal, relying on your own experience, or maybe doing a formal cost-benefit analysis.

One thing you do not want to base important decisions related to risk on are raw emotions, such as anger or fear. Business decisions of any kind should always be made with a clear mind. Any risk you take should not be based on a gamble that relies on pure chance. Again, having accurate and timely information at your disposal is essential.

Plus, anytime you take a risk, be prepared for the potential reward or downside in advance. Determine how you'll proceed, with contingencies based on potential outcomes. It's easier to take risks if your business maintains a financial safety net that can keep your company operational should things not go as planned.

Some people are born risk takers. Others try to avoid risk altogether. Based on my experience, to run a successful business, you need to take risks that make sense but not pursue foolish or irresponsible risks. A balance needs to be achieved. After all, many people are likely counting on you to make the best possible decisions for your business.

So, when approaching any type of risk, my overall advice is to gather information, seek advice when necessary, trust your gut, and focus on your core objectives. Keep a clear head and try to avoid having to make rushed decisions. You're always better off taking your time, looking at situations from different perspectives, and doing what it takes so the probabilities of success become more favorable.

RISK TAKING IS A PART OF BEING A BUSINESS OWNER

Every day of my professional life while I was running a business, I was forced to make all sorts of decisions and take many types of risks. That's part of the job, so prepare for it. Looking back, I may have trusted my gut too much instead of following proven risk analysis or risk management steps.

Keep in mind, in the early days when I was first starting out, there was no internet, we did not have computers on our desks, and there was no digital assistant built into our phones that could provide instant information upon request. If you needed more information, it required doing manual research. This could take a lot of time and require using up resources or manpower. Thanks to today's technological tools, this is no longer the case. A tremendous amount of information, statistics, and data can be collected and analyzed in seconds using the right applications.

My focus was always to take calculated risks, as opposed to simply gambling with my company's future. You might say I had a good personal tolerance for risk, but I wasn't about to put the wellbeing of my company or its employees in jeopardy. One type of risk I was almost never willing to take related to safety. Working with elevators can be very dangerous.

Not being compliant with safety regulations, cutting corners to save money, using inferior parts, taking on the wrong types of jobs, working on elevators I knew were not built properly, or having unqualified employees with an inadequate skillset, could put people in jeopardy—impacting the lives of my employees and the people who would ultimately be riding in the elevators.

Anytime we started a new job in the field, I taught my employees to do a risk assessment of the work location and the equipment. If the location was unsafe, that needed to be addressed before any work on the elevator equipment began.

For example, there was one job we took on that required maintaining the elevators in a hospital. The elevator pit where my employees needed to work was filled with used needles and medical refuse. I insisted that the hospital personnel who were qualified to handle those hazardous materials clean up the worksite before I allowed my employees to do their work. This caused a delay, but the safety of my employees took precedence over the necessity to fix the elevator quickly.

Over the years, I was also cautious about taking financial risks. I never wanted to take on too much debt, spend excessive amounts of money on things we did not absolutely need, or take on large loans that we might have trouble paying back if things didn't go well or there was a downturn in the economy. I relied heavily on my own experience and common sense but also took into consideration advice from my business partners, mentors who worked in the industry, bankers, accountants, lawyers, and my wife.

Because my company has a very positive reputation, from time to time we're offered jobs that are simply too big for us to take on. In these situations, I would weigh the risk of over extending our resources and manpower, versus taking a job that could become profitable.

To take on some of those big jobs, I would need to go to the bank to ask for money to finance the job and pay for the extra employees and equipment we'd need. That meant taking on debt, and then taking on the financial risk knowing that the large job might not go as planned or stay on schedule based on situations that were outside of my control.

On a new building construction, for example, it could take one or more years to get paid. Thus, I needed to consider how we'd bankroll the new job and determine if it was financially worth the risk, while also having to pay interest on the loan we would need to take on.

I tended to be risk adverse when it came to fast company growth, or if I was asked to take a financial risk that was unnecessary for the wellbeing of the company or its long-term viability.

In those situations, I needed to carefully weigh the pros and cons of taking on the larger jobs and the financial risks associated with them. I learned those big jobs could pay off big but could just as easily fall apart and cause us to lose a fortune. Throughout the decades, I saw many of my competitors going bust due to being over-extended or by trying to grow too fast.

I also had to pay attention to the reputation of the company or organization that was offering us the work. If they already had a history for paying bills late, that was a huge red flag for me, so I'd avoid them. There were times when we'd maintain or repair an elevator for a client, but it would break down way too frequently. If the problem was our fault, we'd of course fix the issue immediately.

But anytime the client would insist we did something wrong, we'd study the situation. More often than not, it would turn out that the client's employees or the building's residents were mishandling the elevator.

For example, they'd overload it with too much weight, crash into it with a forklift, or kids would jump up and down in the elevator while it was moving. I'd sometimes have to invest in installing cameras in and around the elevators to prove an elevator's problems were a result of misuse. The client would then need to pay for those repairs. It was my responsibility to avoid difficult clients that wound up taking too much time to coddle and manage.

There were also times when we were offered contracts to maintain elevators in hospitals. Those operations work 24 hours per day, which meant that if an elevator broke, it would need to be fixed immediately and could not wait for the next business day.

Taking on too many of these clients would cause the regular work schedules of our employees to change frequently, and it could dramatically increase our overtime salary costs. And if too many people had to work in the middle of the night, they could not be available the following day. This would cause a manpower shortage. Plus, if an employee had to work extra-long hours and was tired, the chances of making a mistake that could cause injuries increased.

Another way I'd try to mitigate risk is to try to convince clients that were operating old or outdated elevators to invest in newer and more reliable equipment and technologies. If I could do this, it would be easier for us to keep those elevators maintained and running properly, and it was safer for the people who'd be using the client's elevators on a daily basis.

This often meant convincing the client to take on the financial risk of upgrading their equipment. There were also times when a new client would try to hire us to maintain its elevators, but we'd do an evaluation and determine whether the equipment they had already installed, even though it was relatively new, was really poorly made or had a high breakdown rate.

Knowing this, I'd be leery to take on the risk of that new client, since it would require more work on our part to keep those elevators running. Plus, knowing they were potentially dangerous, I did not want to take the risk if the elevators injured someone.

When an elevator make and model is known to have safety issues or be poorly made, even providing the best maintenance can't make them safer or more reliable. As the company that agreed to handle their maintenance, that equipment would become our responsibility. This is another scenario when I'd typically be risk averse and turn down that job or maintenance contract.

Anytime I took a financial risk, I made sure it was not based on greed. Yes, we might be able to make a quick buck, but I needed to determine if over the long term, taking that risk could impact the business' operations in a negative way. I had to consider all angles and potential outcomes.

The risks I was often willing to take involved giving us the opportunity to work with new types of equipment. Once we did that initial job successfully, and learned all about that equipment, we could then expand our service offerings moving forward. That could lead to more revenue and the opportunity to work with a wider range of clients.

My big-picture strategy was always to keep things as simple as possible. I'd be on the lookout for opportunities I believed could transform into something really good. For example, there was one small elevator company that took on a really big job in the territory my company also covers.

The job turned out to be too overwhelming for them, so they wound up in a lot of financial trouble and could not complete the job they were hired to do. I saw this as an opportunity and acquired the company for a very good price. My team was then able to complete the job properly and profitably. It was a win-win situation for everyone involved. For my company, it represented a manageable investment and expansion.

Again, the more information I could gather before taking a risk, the more comfortable I was making decisions. This also dramatically improved the odds for a successful outcome. This strategy applied when I was hiring new elevator mechanics, too. I'd seek out people with experience that came highly recommended, and who had already proven themselves to be competent.

I never wanted to take on the risk of having an unqualified employee, unless we knew this was the case and could provide them with the training they needed before they started work in the field.

There was one case many years ago when I hired someone to be an elevator maintenance person, and it turned out they lied about their qualifications and work history. They had zero experience fixing or maintaining elevators. This was long before we became a union shop. His previous job was as a janitor responsible for cleaning the inside of the elevators. We figured this out within minutes after he arrived at his first field job. He was quickly terminated.

I learned my lesson moving forward and became much more careful when hiring employees and trusting their qualifications. A situation like that never happened again. I have always been unwilling to take the risk of having unqualified or incompetent employees. These days, the union provides proper training above and beyond what an elevator maintenance person or mechanic learns in school.

As a result, when we hire someone who is a union member, we can be more comfortable knowing they're fully qualified. On top of that, we always try to hire new employees based on personal recommendations from people we know and trust. Yet another example when I was hesitant to take a risk is when it came to installing parts or equipment that were new on the market and not yet properly tested in the real world.

I'd love to tell you that risk taking becomes easier over time. In reality, while you may become more experienced when it comes to choosing which risks to take or more adept at deciding on a level of risk you're comfortable with, some risk taking will always be complicated and stressful. This is why having a plan to analyze and manage risk makes so much sense.

To be honest, however, there were times when I needed to decide whether or not to take a risk and to make that decision, I literally just flipped a coin. Of course, I took this approach when the potential for negative consequences was low. A more common approach to risk taking for me was to solicit advice when I needed it, and to rely on my own past experiences.

CREATE A RISK MANAGEMENT PROCESS FOR YOUR BUSINESS

Every business and business operator is different. Thus, it's important for you to develop a risk management process that's suitable for your business and that aligns with your own comfort level in regard to risk taking.

Early on, take the time to identify any potential risks your business might face or be required to take. Then, assess each of those risks and the likelihood of the outcome not going in your favor, and what the severity of the negative outcome could be.

Come up with a defined plan to evaluate and address each risk, so you know what strategies to implement and when. Next, try to implement controls over your risks so you have a contingency plan in place if things go wrong. However, also consider how you'll proceed with a positive outcome.

Over time, risk factors change, so be sure you're making decisions based on current information, trends, and data. What worked a week, month, year, or decade ago may not have the same outcome today. And if things don't go as planned, try to have a safety net in place to mitigate losses, such as the appropriate type of insurance or enough money on hand (or available to your business) to compensate for losses or damages.

Finally, when taking a risk is necessary, consider the short- and long-term ramifications to your business. For example, taking on long-term debt, such as a mortgage or lease, can be problematic, especially for a startup that may experience a few months of lower than expected income. Being late on payments can damage your company's credit rating and ruin your relationship with banks.

PROVEN STRATEGIES FOR APPROACHING DIFFERENT WORK-RELATED RISKS

As I stated earlier, I relied heavily on my gut and common sense when it came to risk taking. Over time, I learned there were additional steps I could take, based on the type of risk, to put the odds more in my favor.

Here are 10 strategies to implement when you're considering taking any type of risk:

1. Gather as much information and data as possible. Ask lots of questions. Look for ways to reduce potential threats and focus on the potential reward.
2. Consider the long-term impact of similar risks you've taken in the past.
3. Pay attention to what your competition is doing (or has done), and factors related to your industry and the economy as a whole.
4. Consult with people you trust, including your mentor, accountants, lawyers, bankers, and relatives who understand your business and the challenges it faces.
5. Create a simple pros and cons list on a sheet of paper. Create two columns and consider the benefits versus the potential pitfalls of taking each risk.
6. Use tech-based risk management and risk assessment tools to gather and analyze data, study trends, and consider options you might not have thought of yourself.
7. Always keep your company's overall goals and vision in mind. When necessary, think outside the box about ways to improve the chances of success when taking a risk.
8. Calculate the chances of your risk turning out the way you want it to, while taking into account both internal and external factors you may or may not have control over.
9. Focus on what true benefits you could experience if the risk works out in your favor, while considering your game plan if the risk doesn't have a positive outcome. Consider doing a cost/benefit analysis and be prepared for whatever happens. Determine if

there's any type of insurance you can put into place if something does not go as you hope.

10. Believe in yourself, your experience, and your knowledge. Trust your gut even if all of the data suggests the risk is acceptable, and the potential for success is good. If something does not feel right, consider why your gut is telling you otherwise.

Once you take a risk, carefully evaluate how things move forward. Be prepared to handle unexpected circumstances and consequences. Keep in mind, there is no cookie-cutter approach to decision making or risk taking for a business operator. Everything must be approached on a case-by-case basis.

Being an owner of a family business, I always needed to consider the ramifications of risk taking and how it might impact my family members. This sometimes made risk taking more of a challenge. After all, if the risk I took wound up losing money, it would impact the business and the personal finances of my relatives who were trusting me to make the best decisions.

PROPER INSURANCE CAN HAVE YOUR BACK WHEN THINGS GO WRONG

There are many types of insurance available that can help manage losses or problems when things do not go as planned. Regardless of what type of business you run, consult with an insurance professional you trust (someone who understands your business), and then invest in the proper types of insurance and appropriate levels of coverage. Don't cut corners to save a few bucks, and if times get tough, don't let the insurance policies lapse. Keep paying those premiums.

Based on your company's unique needs, you might consider acquiring a business owner's policy (BOP), general liability insurance, professional liability coverage, workers' compensation insurance, health insurance (for yourself and your employees), business interruption insurance, commercial property insurance, commercial auto insurance, cyber liability insurance, tools and equipment insurance, directors and officers insurance, commercial umbrella insurance, product liability insurance, home-based business insurance, key person (key executive) insurance, or employer practices liability insurance.

There are also industry-specific types of insurance your business might need or could benefit from. Of course, you will not need every type of insurance listed here, but you want to make sure you're fully covered for the problems your type of business might encounter. Not having proper insurance is taking a big risk unto itself.

Every type of insurance costs money, and its cost is based on a variety of factors, including the level of coverage you require. I've always believed it's important to have adequate insurance. Otherwise, you could be taking a huge risk if something goes wrong and you're forced to cover the financial damages or loss on your own. This could be devastating to your business' financial stability.

Of course, it's also important to establish your business as the right type of legal entity, whether it's a sole proprietorship, partnership, LLC, nonprofit, or some type of corporation. Each offers specific types of financial and legal protections if things go wrong.

I suggest speaking with a lawyer and accountant as you're first starting your business to make sure you make the right decisions, as this can have financial, tax, and legal ramifications moving forward.

IT TAKES MORE THAN SMART RISK TAKING TO GROW A BUSINESS

Since every business is different, I've tried to share my own experiences but cater my advice so it relates to any type of business that's operating in any industry. In the next chapter, I will share more of my experience taking over Embree Elevator and growing it into the successful family-owned business that it's become today.

My goal is to help you avoid some of the mistakes I made early on and provide guidance so you can more easily overcome some of the challenges I faced. I'll also discuss a few strategies that worked particularly well for me over the past few decades working as an entrepreneur.

For me, learning to be an entrepreneur and successful business operator has been a life-long endeavor. It required me to obtain updated knowledge and skills as my company grew, my industry evolved, and the world as a whole changed. To be a successful entrepreneur, never stop learning and evolving.

Remember, you should never be content with your existing knowledge and experience, as the world around you and the challenges you'll face will continuously be changing. Once you stop growing as a person, you'll be putting yourself and your business at a huge disadvantage.

4

Founding and Growing Embree Elevator

"Your work is going to fill a large part of your life, and the only way to be truly satisfied is to do what you believe is great work."

STEVE JOBS

HAVING WORKED for other employers and seeing my father work so hard for his employers for so many years, I wanted something different. In addition to being able to control my own professional destiny, I wanted the financial rewards, decision-making ability, and other benefits for myself and my family that go along with running your own business and being the boss.

MY THIRD BUSINESS IS MORE THAN 53 YEARS OLD AND STILL GOING STRONG

By the time my business partner, wife, and I bought and took over Embree Elevator in 1972, we were ready to transform it into the multi-generational family business it is today. I was 42 years old at the time. I already had plenty of experience working as an employee for other companies when I was younger.

I also had my military experience and spent years running two other businesses in the elevator industry—Payne Elevator (1955 to 1968) and City Elevator (1969 to 1972). My first professional experience working with elevators happened when I was 19 years old, back in July 1950. Before that, my dad took me to some of his onsite jobs while I was growing up. He's the one who taught me so much about working with my hands and about building and repairing mechanical stuff.

As you already know, I grew up having an entrepreneurial spirit and a strong work ethic that I learned from my father. In other words, when we took over Embree Elevator, I was experienced enough to know what I was getting into. I had realistic expectations. I also already had the core skillset and business knowledge needed to develop a strategy and set realistic goals starting the day we took over.

In addition to combining my own knowledge and experience with what my partner and wife brought to the table, we did not hesitate to seek out guidance from a variety of bankers, lawyers, accountants, insurance agents, and business consultants, including that guy I referenced to earlier who was one of the driving forces behind the success of Dunkin' Donuts.

These days, business professionals network more on LinkedIn than they do in person. My networking back then all happened in person and by landline telephone. If handled correctly, the end result can be the same. Gather a group of knowledgeable people whom you trust and can turn to when you have questions or issues with which they can potentially help.

I also had many friends in the elevator industry who were happy to share advice and answer my questions. For example, I sought advice from a former executive with Otis Elevator. He was a friend. I asked him for the most important advice he could offer, and his response was "insurance." He said that not only do you want to be covered if someone is actually injured on the job, but you need to be prepared if people try to fake an injury and want a financial settlement.

All these years later, I have become a firm believer in insurance, although it's harder to get good coverage, especially workers compensation insurance, when your company relies on people doing dangerous jobs involving fast-moving machinery and electricity, in tight spaces like an elevator shaft. It's required some extra effort over the years to ensure we worked with the best insurance providers.

FOR ME, IT'S ALWAYS BEEN SAFETY FIRST

Throughout the decades, as I was assigning each employee their tasks for the day, I would reiterate that they should be safe. Then, once every month, we'd gather all of the employees and review all of the latest safety regulations in person.

Volunteering my time to be part of the state's Elevator Safety Board and the National Review Board allowed me to stay on top of all of the latest safety protocols and procedures related to my industry. I was then able to share that information with my employees. I firmly believe that my insistence on safety has helped to prevent many injuries and potential deaths over the years, and I am proud of that.

HAVING A BUSINESS PARTNER OFFERS A DIFFERENT POINT OF VIEW

One reason why I chose my last business partner was because he had a different set of ideas than I did, but we agreed on the big picture for the business. I figured that having someone by my side with different ideas (that stemmed from having a different background and work experiences) could be very useful. It turned out I was right about that.

Since we were using our own money to buy and fund the business initially, there was no need to create a formal business plan. In retrospect, we probably should have. Much of what would have been included in a business plan was covered during in-depth brainstorming and business planning conversations between myself, my business partner, and my wife. The information was just never put into a single document.

IT'S IMPOSSIBLE TO IGNORE TECHNOLOGY IN THE 21ST CENTURY

Today, there are websites and computer applications that allow an entrepreneur to create a detailed, professional, and nicely formatted business plan rather quickly, simply by answering a bunch of questions and choosing a template that fits the type of business being created. Those tools did not exist back in 1972, but I would highly recommend using them today.

In fact, there are all sorts of internet and software-based tools that make it so much easier to run a business and keep everything well organized and documented. This includes partially automating things like bookkeeping and maintaining financial records, team scheduling, risk management and risk assessment, handling customer service, performing HR-related tasks, inventory management, and so much more.

I've seen technology progress so much and so fast during my lifetime. I recommend taking advantage of it whenever you can, as long as it makes sense to do so. That said, while I was writing this book, one of the most popular buzzwords in the business world was "artificial intelligence."

Honestly, I am not sure how I feel about this technology. It was not around when I was handling the day-to-day operations of my business, but it's certainly something my daughter has to deal with now that she's in charge.

My fear about artificial intelligence is that it could make people lazy. The next generations may not have the wherewithal to develop a true work ethic or interpersonal communication skills. They could wind up relying too much on AI for so many things. In my opinion, this can be dangerous for business and society at large.

SUCCESS IS MULTIFACETED

I can't pinpoint one specific thing that made my business successful. Success, no matter how you define it, is built on everything from strong communication and knowledge building to solid procedures and protocols. I built my career around developing and maintaining personal relationships with my employees, clients, and suppliers. We maintained an open line of communication, either in person or by phone. My employees were always welcome to knock on my door if they had any issues or suggestions.

For a business leader who has not built this type of rapport with their employees, I recommend offering a suggestion box. This could allow people to share their complaints or ideas anonymously if they choose to yet help to maintain open communication. It also shows you care about your employees and their thoughts.

Today, with so many other technology-based ways to communicate that are far less personal, I fear that the importance of maintaining relationships in business will deteriorate. At least for now, however, I truly believe that building and maintaining in person relationships is still critical for an entrepreneur's success.

I'd like to reiterate that I did not graduate from college. And since I was working so hard, six days a week for most of my adult life, I never had time to read business books to help expand my knowledge. Mostly, I learned from other people, by attending industry trade shows, and from hands-on experience.

Back in the day, we often solved problems using a simple trial and error approach. If something did not work, we'd try something else. The trick was having the courage to try new things and never give up easily. For me that worked, but in today's business world, I think having a formal education is important. But even once you graduate, you should never stop learning.

As part of the Elevator Safety Board and National Elevator Review Board, one of our responsibilities was to write and continuously update a safety protocol code book which related to all elevators. It covers elevators that were installed more than 100 years ago (which are still operational), and the most cutting-edge elevators that are now controlled using computers.

This elevator code and regulations book that I helped to create and continue to help update is now several inches thick. It's also something I refer back to often, since I have input into what changes need to be made based on new elevator designs and technologies. We also take into account injuries that have occurred and try to figure out ways to prevent similar problems in the future on an industry-wide basis.

Sometimes, to get new safety protocols or policies passed, it requires dealing with a lot of politics and pushback from the elevator manufacturers, landlords, companies with elevators in their buildings, as well as politicians, union reps, and others with a vested interest in the elevator industry.

Some of these protocols determine how often an elevator needs to be tested and have maintenance work done on it. The landlords and building owners with elevators are the ones who pay for the state-mandated inspection fees, so while we pushed for testing and maintenance to be done often, they want less-frequent requirements to save money. These days, a basic maintenance check or inspection can cost $400 per elevator. That adds up quickly for a landlord who owns multiple buildings, each with a bunch of elevators within them.

Learning to navigate these politics helped me develop negotiation and other skills that were useful to running my own business. I also learned a lot about being persistent to get what I wanted or needed in the business world.

YES, THE CUSTOMER REALLY IS ALWAYS RIGHT

Another lesson I learned was based on a common saying in the business world. It also proved itself to be useful. That is, "The customer is always right." When there's a problem, straighten it out. Never walk away from it or burn bridges. When you make a situation right, the customer or client will remember you and stay more loyal to you.

Anytime an issue arose, I'd ask what the client wanted or needed, and then listen carefully. I'd try to determine what the real underlying problem was. Sometimes, it took a few minutes to get down to what was really wrong. Then, I tried offering one or more solutions that made sense, and that would satisfy everyone. A few times, I even offered to hire a competitor to come in and do the required work instead.

Reaching an agreement became much easier once the client knew they were being heard. There were also times when I relied on my sense of humor to lighten a tense situation. Even if we ultimately had to part ways, I never did this in a way that the client remained angry or disappointed.

In the instances when I could not get through to a client and reach an agreement, I'd have my business partner step in. He had a different personality and would take a different approach. Sometimes that did the trick.

One thing that set Embree Elevator apart from competitors was our philosophy related to helping a client keep their existing elevators running as long as possible, as long as they remained safe. We still made money doing the maintenance and repairs, as opposed to selling them all new equipment.

Meanwhile, our competitors would often try to sell their clients new and more modern elevators, which was much more expensive. Again, by looking out for our clients' best interests, this helped us build a good reputation and keep those clients for many years—sometimes decades.

Earlier, I talked about how when Embree Elevator became a union shop, we were forced to raise our rates rather dramatically. For a while during that transition, it was only because we had loyal clients and good relationships with them that they stayed with us. This kept us in business during what was a difficult financial time for us.

Back then, I remember telling one of our long-time clients that we'd need to raise their rates. He actually thanked me for doing this. He knew it would keep us in business, and he wanted us to be the company that kept his elevators operational, just as we had done for years. He had already proven our value to him. We were always very loyal, and when we needed his loyalty, he had no trouble providing it.

ALWAYS DEMONSTRATE RESPECT, ADAPTABILITY, AND KINDNESS

The concept of "respect" has played a large role in my success throughout my professional life. I always showed the utmost respect for coworkers, bosses, and later my own employees, customers, clients, suppliers, and anyone else I came into contact with in a professional capacity.

First, I'd try to earn someone's respect, and I'd look for ways to respect them. Everyone has their own background, experience, skillset, personality, and belief system. The key is to try to get along with everyone in business and avoid focusing on how people are different from you. Focus on what you have in common. For me, taking a very open and honest approach with all my interactions has served me well. Kindness has always been a key part of my personality, too.

People who look at my past can easily see that I constantly showed respect, kindness, and generosity to the people around me, and to my industry as a whole, the union, and the people I came into contact with in my everyday life.

This extended into my personal life, too. I also consistently showed respect, kindness, and loyalty to my family, friends, community, country, and my church, for example. In other words, I was always consistent. This too is something I initially learned from my parents.

Another personality trait that I think is important for an entrepreneur is adaptability. In my work, my clients are mostly business executives, landlords, or real estate owners, for example. They're business oriented, intelligent, typically wear suits, and are often well educated. My employees are mostly skilled tradespeople who work with their hands. Most went to trade school, not business school. They lead a totally different lifestyle.

My job always involved getting along with these two distinct groups and finding ways they could seamlessly coexist in each other's worlds when my employees were working on site within the buildings owned by the clients. Looking back, I think I did a good job with this. In addition to having clients that have been with us for decades, we have employees that have been with us for just as long.

One of our employees has been with us for more than 40 years. His two sons now work for us also. I believe loyalty and respect are valuable. If you demonstrate your loyalty and respect, people will typically be loyal and respectful to you. Sometimes, that can last beyond one generation.

And when you keep clients and employees for so long, you save a lot of time, money, and effort over the long term. There's little need to continuously spend time and resources having to find and land new clients or have to seek out new and well-qualified employees. The time and money that would otherwise be spent on those tasks were reallocated elsewhere.

How I communicated with my clients was often very different from the way I'd address my employees. This requires a lot of adaptability, patience, and understanding. Also, you need to be able to look beyond your own ego and determine when you need to take a different approach to something or change strategies altogether.

We are all living in a world that's constantly changing. The needs of customers change. Industries change. The economy goes up and down. Trends are always coming and going. When you study trends for a while, you can often determine which ones will last and could have an impact on your business.

As a business operator, not only do you need to stay aware of these changes and adapt to them, but you also need to find ways to capitalize on them whenever possible. Embrace change when necessary; don't fight it. Not everyone likes having to deal with change of any kind. These people can get stuck in their same old ways of doing things. This approach will no longer work in business.

Ultimately, no matter what type of business you plan to run (or are already running), you need to have the guts to try new things, and when necessary, take risks. When I took over Embree Elevator, I had four young children to support. It was a rather significant risk, but I knew I wanted to be able to provide a good life for them. My kids became one of my motivations to work hard and strive for success.

Having confidence in yourself, without being arrogant, is also an important personality trait. That said, when it came to growing my business I've always adopted a slow and steady approach. For example, once we chose what geographic area Embree Elevator would cover, we pretty much stuck with it. I always tried to thread the needle between being confident and careful.

Only a few times over the years did we expand out beyond that area and only did so when it made really good business and financial sense to do so. I never wanted to open satellite offices to cater to a larger area. That would have been too hard for me to manage. It also would have kept me from conducting business the way I wanted to. All my business-related goals were always realistic.

LIFE AND WORK REQUIRE OVERCOMING MANY CHALLENGES

Three of the most challenging events in my personal life have been the loss of my wife after 66 years of marriage, the rocky relationship I have with one of my sons, and most recently, the sudden death of my granddaughter.

My son is not currently married and has no children. Among other things, we don't see eye-to-eye on a variety of issues, including his work ethic. I really hope to improve my relationship with him before it's too late.

Many years after I unofficially retired, another huge emotional challenge was the loss of my granddaughter. She was Carol's daughter and lived next door to me. I got to see her grow up and was privileged to spend so much time with her. She accomplished more in her 30 years of life than most people who live to 100. She loved the outdoors, was a master scuba diver, and global traveler. She put her skills to work doing all sorts of impactful charity work around the world. Her life's mission was to help people and animals.

In 2024, she was diagnosed with acute myeloid leukemia and succumbed to it rather quickly, despite having the best medical care. This loss was a huge blow to everyone in my extended family, and something we're all still trying to come to terms with.

Professionally, my biggest challenge was making the transition when Embree Elevator became a union shop. I have always respected the union and continue to support it, but the financial ramifications of becoming a union shop almost destroyed my business. For me, that was a very difficult time financially and psychologically.

Another major challenge occurred when my business partner, John McHugh, retired. Finding someone to take on his responsibilities was difficult. He was the best business partner I ever had, a great person to be around, and a superior mechanic. We also shared the same family values. He too had a long-lasting marriage, plus he had six children. Two of his daughters worked in the business when they were in high school, but all of his kids eventually pursued their own careers.

In 1996, when John retired, Virginia and I then bought out his share of the business. I had to promote an employee who previously worked in the field and bring him into the office. I then needed to train him to handle new responsibilities. I did not previously have a plan to take on the responsibilities of my business partner. After he decided to retire, he left the company very quickly.

Later, after my daughter and then my son-in-law joined the business and ultimately became the vice president and chief financial officer, respectively, I was able to delegate a lot to them. We also worked as a team when we had to deal with larger company challenges. Each of us have different personalities, experiences, and backgrounds. This coming together as a trio really helped the business prosper.

Thus, when I was ready to turn over the operation of the business to my daughter, the transition was easier. Carol had already been with the company for fifteen years, so she was prepared to take on the additional responsibilities. She's always been a good business woman, and I have always been very confident in her abilities.

Yet another thing I found challenging while I was running the business was determining exactly when it was time to bring on additional employees and expand, without over-extending ourselves. Again, my approach was always slow and steady. In addition to what was going on within my business, I paid careful attention to industry trends, and the strength of the national economy.

Today, technology can analyze data and help you crunch numbers quickly when making almost any type of business decisions. I recommend using those tools because it makes things so much easier, compared to the days when we did not have access to computers.

The problem with major personal or professional challenges is that they're always on your mind. It's difficult to put those thoughts aside so you can focus better on the tasks at hand. Learning to be able to focus on your daily responsibilities while facing a challenge can be very difficult.

The thing about facing challenges and living through difficult times and loss is that it forces you to better appreciate all of the good that life has to offer. It also makes you grateful for what you have and better appreciate experiences from your past.

Whenever I've had to endure the loss of someone close to me, it's forced me to consider how I existed in the world prior to them entering my life and allowed me to reflect on all of the ways that person enriched my life while they were in it. The one drawback to living beyond 95 years old is that you're forced to deal with a lot of major challenges and personal loss. Unfortunately, it never gets easier.

FIVE STEPS FOR DEALING WITH WORK-RELATED CHALLENGES

As a business operator, I discovered unexpected challenges arise regularly and often when you least expect them. Some you can plan for, but most you cannot. Anytime I was faced with a business-related challenge, most of the time I'd follow these five steps:

1. Try to figure out what got us into that situation. In other words, identify the core issue.
2. Determine the issue's impact on the business.
3. While maintaining a calm attitude, brainstorm solutions for the problem and then choose the best option. When necessary, I'd consult with your support system to get their ideas and advice, too.
4. After creating an action plan, I'd do what's necessary to fix the problem and overcome the challenge. To accomplish this, I'd use the resources at my disposal in the most efficient way possible.
5. Clean up the mess, recover from any types of losses, and then learn as much as possible from the experience. My goal was never to repeat a similar experience in the future.

One thing to keep in mind is that when you're the boss, people look up to you and expect you to define the company's culture, provide solutions to problems, maintain a professional demeanor and avoid emotional outbursts, regardless of the situation.

To solve certain issues or overcome various problems might require you to change the way things have been done in the past and adopt new strategies. Be open to this and don't be afraid of change. Just make sure all your employees stay well informed and on the same page to make transitions happen smoothly.

Dealing with problems and challenges can take an emotional toll, but I learned it's very important to keep personal emotions in check and to face issues with a clear head. Take emotions out of the equation as much as possible.

Being an entrepreneur and business operator can be stressful. It's important to learn how to deal with and manage that stress so it doesn't become overwhelming or debilitating. For me, that meant working out at the gym every weekday morning at 5:00am. Most nights, to relax and end my day, I would sit on the couch with my wife, and we'd watch light-hearted TV shows together.

Everyone has to find their own solution for clearing their head and dealing with stress. Figure out early on what works for you and then make the time to regularly follow that stress reduction or elimination strategy. When people fail at this, I've seen them ruin their life and career by turning to drugs, alcohol, or gambling.

In your life, don't allow your stress level to reach the point where this could happen. Try to catch the signs of a problem early on and then be brave enough to seek whatever help you need when you need it. Do not wait until it's too late.

MOST PEOPLE DON'T START OFF AS A CEO

As my children and later my grandchildren grew up, I've been able to share plenty of advice about how to prepare for life beyond high school, college, or trade school. In the next chapter, I'll be sharing similar advice with people first kicking off their career.

After all, before you can be the CEO, become an amazing boss, and do a great job choosing and managing employees (which is what I cover in Chapter 6, "How to Become an Amazing Boss and Manage Employees"), you need to build a strong foundation for yourself and career. This includes figuring out where your passions lie and learning how to set realistic short-term and long-term goals for yourself.

THIS PAGE, CLOCKWISE FROM LEFT: *Virginia Comley and James F. Comley receive UMass Lowell Honory Alumni Award; Virginia and James F. Comley wedding; Virginia and James F. Comley wedding vow renewal on 60th anniversary*

FACING PAGE, CLOCKWISE FROM TOP LEFT: *Paddle boarding, summer 2023; 2011 Ellis Island Medal of Honor award recipient; James Comley with an 1890 flat belt machine, before it was shipped to the Elevator Museum; James F. Comley in US Navy*

Virginia and James Comley in front of their Bedford home, the historic Elijah Stearns Mansion

Virginia and James Comley on their 66th wedding anniversary

James and Virginia Comley with their children, Michael, Bonnie, Stephen, and Carol

James Comley and family, 2026

James Comley, John McHugh

James Comley with Embree Elevator vans

Embree Executive Leadership: James Comley, Carol Washer, Cliff Washer

Embree Elevator team

Jake Comley, Stephen Comley, James Comley, and David Morgan, Executive Director of the National Elevator Industry Educational Program (NEIEP)

Scott Hult, Cliff Washer, Gary Sawyer, James Comley, Michael Lucey, David Lucey

5

My Advice to Those First Starting Out

> *"There are no secrets to success. It is the result of preparation, hard work, and learning from failure."*
>
> COLIN POWELL

SINCE I BECAME an adult so many decades ago, I can't recall exactly how many times I'd experience something and think to myself, "I wish someone told me about this when I was younger." Well, in this chapter, I am looking back and reflecting on the useful information, life lessons, and advice that I can share now, but that I didn't necessarily have while growing up.

Much of what's in this chapter is information and advice I've shared with my own children and later my grandchildren as they were growing up. Thus, it will appeal to people first graduating from high school, trade school, or college, who might not have figured out what professional interests to pursue, or what type of career track they should follow.

Based on my life experience, knowing what you want out of life, having clearly defined goals, and putting together well-thought-out strategies for achieving those life and career objectives is important. I believe everyone should follow their passions and focus on their strengths (what they're good at) when it comes to choosing jobs or ultimately a career.

PURSUE WORK THAT MAKES YOU TRULY HAPPY

Attending college can open your eyes to a world filled with opportunities you might not otherwise know existed, but that's not an educational path everyone chooses to pursue. The good news is you can still attend job fairs and industry trade shows. And there are always ways you can pivot. You can earn promotions and work your way up within a company, as you simultaneously learn more about an industry. Or you can change jobs or careers if you discover better opportunities elsewhere and your interests change over time.

I've always encouraged my children and grandchildren to pursue a career that would make them happy. In other words, I never expected them to join the family business, unless it was something they clearly wanted to do. I know there are parents out there who put a lot of pressure on their kids to follow in their footsteps, but your life is your own. You should take on jobs and pursue a career that makes you happy, that you find rewarding, and that will allow you to live the life you want to live.

Anytime you can pursue a job or career you love, you'll have a much easier time waking up every morning and being excited to go to work. And when you're happy on the job, you'll have an easier time succeeding at it, even if it requires long hours and hard work. So, my first and most important piece of advice for someone first entering the workforce is to find the skills and things you are good at, and you will become excited and passionate about being challenged and learning more.

Next, even if you're now well educated, as someone first starting out in the workforce, remember that you lack real-world experience. If your goal is to someday launch your own business, first invest time working for another company. Learn as much as you can about how that business operates.

Also learn everything possible about that industry, the companies working in that industry, the size of the marketplace, and how the other successful businesses in that industry operate. Study trends, get to know the ins and outs of the business's operation, its suppliers (if applicable), its customers, and try to determine what it's doing right, and what you think the business's owners are doing wrong.

WHEN TO CONSIDER STARTING YOUR OWN BUSINESS

Only once you have plenty of real-world experience working in a specific industry should you enter it as a business owner by attempting to launch your own business. When you do, have a very clearly defined plan.

Step one after you choose what type of business you want to create and launch is to compose a detailed business plan. Then, line up the required financing, and establish realistic short- and long-term goals for your company. Plenty of planning and research will help you achieve success. Start with a strong business foundation. This is not the time to rush things or cut corners.

Understand that owning your own business is far more complicated than being an employee and working for someone else's company. Far more responsibilities fall onto your shoulders as a business owner. You'll also need to juggle many responsibilities at the same time and master all of the skills necessary to run the business' day-to-day operations. It will be necessary to figure out how to attract customers/clients and be able to do things better than your competition.

This means learning absolutely everything there is to know about the products and/or services you plan to offer, and the customers/clients to whom you'll be catering. At the same time, study your competition. Notice and understand new trends happening within your industry. Knowing that things change constantly, it's essential to stay up-to-day and well informed.

And, as I've mentioned numerous times, being a successful entrepreneur and business owner is all about building and maintaining relationships. So, to develop these relationships, make sure you have the verbal and written communication skills and listening skills needed.

Understand why these skills are so important and become comfortable using them. You should easily be able to communicate clearly in-person, on the phone, and via email or text message. Proper phone etiquette is as important as acting professionally when you're face-to-face with someone.

Even if you did not go to college (like me), there are plenty of ways to acquire and master the skills needed to run a business. You can take online classes, read books, or learn from mentors, for example. Back in the day, I took a learn-as-you-go and trial-and-error approach. Today, those strategies won't always cut it. College isn't for everyone but learning to run a business before you actually start one is a very important step, especially in today's cut-throat, technology-oriented business world.

DISCOVER YOUR INTERESTS AND DECIDE WHAT TO PURSUE PROFESSIONALLY

As someone is growing up, I think they should try different things and experience various types of jobs. Very few people can choose a career as a young person that they absolutely love and then stick with it until they're ready to retire.

When I was young, I tried several different types of jobs. For example, I worked in a mill and greenhouse. Watching plants grow was just too slow for me. It was my father who introduced me to one of his friends who worked in the elevator business. He agreed to hire me. That job really piqued my interest.

Each time I went on site to maintain, repair, or replace an elevator, I was exposed to a different industry and met new and interesting people. However, once I actually started working on elevators, nothing else captured my interest. I liked going to work every morning. Each day I experienced something different. I wound up working for a handful of different people in the elevator industry, and learned important things related to this career from all of them.

Working with elevators was exciting for me because every elevator I worked on was different. You could have two elevators side-by-side, but they sometimes functioned differently. There was always something new to learn, things to figure out, new equipment to work with, and interesting things to try.

For me, determining what was wrong with an elevator, and then learning how to fix it was very fascinating, enjoyable, and challenging. Even when an elevator was working, I had to inspect each of them properly every two or three months. During each inspection, I had to look for small clues, predict what could go wrong, and then prevent that from happening.

This meant looking for small oil leaks, identifying worn-down parts, listening for unusual sounds, and feeling vibrations that should not exist.

It was all about observation. If I stepped into an elevator cab and heard loud music playing, I knew there must be something wrong and that the music was turned up on purpose to hide the bad sound the elevator was making.

I was always very good at inspecting elevators and finding small problems before they became big ones. I became a very detail-oriented person, even without realizing it. That's what the job required.

I never got bored with the job. That's how I knew it should become my career. Back when I was first starting out, working on elevators was more dangerous than it is today (even though there's still a lot of risk involved). I think part of me liked the thrill of the job—knowing there was some potential danger.

Regardless of what job or career you step into as a young person, it should be something you enjoy and are qualified to do.

BECOME PROFICIENT WITH TECHNOLOGY

These days, I also suggest that people truly understand how to use technology and their smartphones as the versatile and powerful communication tools they are. And for almost all jobs these days, knowing how to operate a computer proficiently is a must.

I never became as tech savvy as I would have liked, because computers became commonplace as my career was winding down. I had other people who studied computers and knew how to operate them, so I delegated that work to them.

However, I use a smartphone and am rather good at utilizing most of its advanced features. Not too many 95 year olds can say that. I have always been excited by new technologies and their potential.

CONTINUE EXPANDING YOUR PROFESSIONAL SKILLSET

If you plan to be a manager or a boss, having strong communication and listening skills are equally important. But, if you plan to work for someone else, there are plenty of jobs that don't involve you having to interact with other people. You just need to be able to listen and take direction.

Regardless of the job you choose, figure out what skills you'll need, and then take it upon yourself to master those skills so you can become really good at your job.

Employers notice when someone excels at the job they have. Those are the first people who are considered for a raise or promotion. With a promotion comes more responsibility and the need to master additional skills. This makes you more valuable as an employee. If you're constantly working toward the next promotion, you'll often climb up the proverbial corporate ladder faster.

Eventually, you may discover that you're ready to take on the responsibility of launching your own business. However, for many people, it's just as acceptable to spend their career working for another employer. This avoids the added challenges and risks of being a business owner. Again, it all comes down to what you want to accomplish and how hard you're willing to work.

YOUR APPEARANCE IS ALWAYS IMPORTANT ON THE JOB

One thing that few schools teach is how to act on the job. You may have mastered the skills needed to do a job, but you also need to dress and act accordingly. I've seen plenty of young people show up for work without their shirt tucked in, or with their pants falling too low. I've also seen people show up without having paid attention to personal grooming or hygiene. That shows a lack of professionalism.

Even if you're a tradesperson, use common sense and show up wearing a clean uniform. This includes wearing proper shoes for the job you'll be doing—whether you're working in an office, in a retail store, within a factory or warehouse, or out in the field.

You need to look and act presentable. If your boss needs to tell you to dress more presentably and manage your personal grooming or hygiene better (by brushing your hair or taking a shower), you're doing something wrong. Whatever you do for work, show up wearing clean clothes every day and present the best version of yourself to your colleagues and clients.

Also, even if you graduated at the top of your class from a fancy college, don't start a new job thinking and acting like you know more than your boss or the business owner. Having textbook smarts is different from the real-world smarts you can only learn through hands-on experience doing whatever your job entails. When you act arrogant as a new employee, that's a huge red flag for your boss. That type of attitude could also turn your coworkers against you.

Being a friendly person on the job, especially when you're first starting out, will open up more doors for you. Your superiors will be more likely to help you, teach you, and enjoy being around you. Learning to get along with people, even if you don't like them, is an important skill. You should also be respectful of the people you work with and anyone else your job requires you to come into contact with.

MONEY SHOULD NOT BE YOUR ONLY MOTIVATION

One mistake I see a lot of young people make is that as soon as they land a decently paying job, they start spending lots of money on things they don't need. For example, if you want to buy a new car, you don't have to start with a Mercedes. Until you know you have a stable and long-term career, be conservative with your frivolous spending.

If you follow business news on any given day, you'll hear about lots of companies doing mass layoffs, even when the company itself is profitable, and the economy is strong. It's even worse when companies are cutting costs and downsizing to survive. Especially when you're dealing with medium-to-large companies, they're not typically going to let you go with a lot of advanced notice, nor will they help you land a new job quickly.

For this reason, you should always have some extra cash stashed away for times when you really need it. One set of skills that I recommend all young people learn is how to manage their own personal finances and credit responsibility. Credit card debt or over-extending yourself with a rent/mortgage payment or car payment that's too high based on what you earn can lead to long-term financial problems.

You don't need to become a financial or personal investment genius but developing basic personal finance knowledge and understanding how a credit score and your credit rating is calculated, for example, can be very beneficial as you go through life.

TAKE YOUR WORK RESPONSIBILITIES SERIOUSLY

Another complaint I have about young people first entering the workforce is that they don't always take their job seriously. Showing up late, taking extra-long breaks, leaving early at the end of the day, or asking for lots of extra days off is not the way you should present yourself, regardless of your job.

When someone consistently shows up for work on time and is ready to go, that says a lot to a boss. It's something I always noticed and respected. When someone does not put in their full eight hour workday, I consider that dishonesty. The person is being paid for a day's work. If they're not providing that, but being paid for it, that's tantamount to stealing from the employer.

Regardless of what type of work you do, you'll be given responsibilities. These days, companies try to get the most out of each employee as possible, and with cutbacks, will hire fewer people to do more work. Even if the work is being piled on, don't rush through it. If you're in too much of a hurry, you're likely to start making mistakes.

When a company hires you, it's counting on you to perform the tasks you're being paid to do, when you're asked to do them. If your supervisor, manager, or boss needs to track you down, or you don't consistently show up to work, you'll be considered unreliable and run the risk of getting fired.

Keep in mind, it's someone's job at the company you work for to coordinate employee scheduling. If you make that person's job harder by being a flake, it will be held against you. This may seem like common sense, but you'd be surprised how many people simply don't get it.

Depending on the type of position you hold, most employers want employees who can understand and follow directions. However, they don't want robots. People must be able to think for themselves when it comes to making certain types of decisions. If you're holding down a job that involves being part of a union, make sure you understand what that entails. Be sure to follow the union's rules and regulations but also listen to your employer. It's like having two bosses.

Attend the regularly scheduled union meetings. You'll find that your union also teaches classes or workshops. Take part in those, so you can enhance your skillset. This will make you more valuable to your employer.

Union members are a team. But, even if you're not part of a union, when you're working for an employer or at any company that's not your own, you need to be a team player. If you're working on a project that involves a few other people, your job on the team is never to sit back, relax, and watch your other coworkers do the work.

Remember, you're being paid to do work. If nobody assigns you a specific task, find something constructive to do, or ask your supervisor. If you wait around until someone tells you specifically what to do, you'll likely be perceived as being a lazy person.

Plus, if you're in the process of learning a new trade and working as an intern or apprentice, you're not going to fully learn anything until you do it for yourself. If during the learning process you're afraid to mess things up, ask someone for clear directions as you get started with something new, and if you run into problems, ask for help overcoming the situation.

Ultimately, you need to do your job correctly, and make sure it actually gets finished. You don't want someone else to have to step in and deal with any loose ends of a project that you failed to complete. When someone else needs to step in and redo or finish your work, that costs your employer money. It also lowers your value as an employee.

Taking shortcuts on the job demonstrates a poor work ethic. But, as I've discussed several times in this book, having a really good work ethic is what will ultimately help you succeed in the business world, regardless of your job. Also, even if you don't plan to stick with your current employer for a long time, remain loyal. Appreciate the job you have while you have it but focus on moving to the next step in your career.

AVOID BURNING BRIDGES WHEN LEAVING A JOB

Even if you absolutely hate your current boss or employer, refrain from posting negative information online. This makes you look bad and can hinder your ability to land a new job. After all, if a potential new employer sees you've bad-mouthed your past employer in a public online forum, such as your social media feed, they'll be very hesitant to hire you. This is true even if you're otherwise fully qualified for the job you've applied for.

Anytime you say something bad about your boss or employer, assume it will get back to them. Word-of-mouth travels quickly, and there's no such thing as total privacy online.

As someone who's been a boss for decades, I've seen the work ethic of young people as a whole get worse. I suggest you stand out from the crowd and showcase a really strong work ethic if you want to get ahead in your career. My advice when you start any project is to finish it by making things better. Simply completing a task or project isn't good enough.

For example, I've always taught my employees that after they finish a job repairing an elevator, they should sweep up and clean whatever mess they made while doing their work. They should leave the work area cleaner and safer than when they got there, in addition to completing the necessary repairs. This philosophy applies to almost any type of work. Details matter. Take those few extra minutes to make sure you're leaving something better than when you started.

TIPS AND STRATEGIES FOR JOB SEEKERS

Anytime you're applying for a new job, three things I suggest you look for from a potential employer are fair pay, a safe place to work, and that you can have a future working for that company. Knowing what your long-term career goals are determines how much upward mobility there will be for you at the company you're applying to work at.

If you discover that many of the employees working for that company have been there for 30 or 40 years, that's a really good sign. Meanwhile, you should be wary of a company that has a lot of employee turnover.

During job interviews, focus on describing your skills, education, and qualifications. Demonstrate your personality and communication skills. By sharing examples, focus on showcasing your work ethic and accomplishments. But be careful about sharing too much personal information. Also, maintain eye contact, respond with a pleasant demeanor, make sure you're dressed appropriately, and perform the proper personal grooming before the interview..

Avoid bringing up salary and compensation. Wait for the potential employer to broach this topic. Then, learn as much as possible about the base salary, opportunities for overtime, whether it's possible to earn bonuses, and what benefits are part of the overall compensation package.

Remember, most benefits have a monetary value, so look for benefits that appeal to you, and that you'll be able to take advantage of if you accept the job. If part of a benefits package is time off for maternity leave or free pet insurance, but you have no plans to have children and don't have pets, these benefits won't be useful to you. But you might find the ability to take extra personal days or paid vacation days to be a great perk. And think about how much money you'll save if the employer pays for your lunches or commuting costs, for example.

If you're applying for a union job, salary and benefits are spelled out clearly by the union. For non-union jobs, do research to discover what the average salary is for the position you're applying for, in the geographic region where you'll be working.

Next, be ready to ask insightful questions about the position you're applying for and about the company as a whole. Try to determine how strong the company is, and how it's positioned in its industry. As you ask these questions, demonstrate that you've cared enough to do some initial research about the company. Show genuine interest in the position you're applying for.

As someone who has hired many employees over the years, if two applicants interview for the same position and have very similar skills, experience, and education, the applicant I will typically hire is the one who seems like they'd stick with the company for a long time, and who's looking to advance their career.

I do not want to invest the time and resources training someone new, only to have them quit and go work for the competition after a year or two. Another thing I look for is an upbeat and positive personality. Nobody wants to work with a grouch.

Once you have a job and you've been consistently performing well at it, there will be a time when it's appropriate to ask for a raise or promotion. My suggestion is wait until you've had a big win on the job or achieved something major. Be ready to demonstrate your performance and success in quantifiable and qualitative terms. Never give an ultimatum, like "Give me a raise, or I quit."

Especially when you're first starting out in the real world, you're going to have a lot of questions. I suggest finding one or more mentors who can provide insightful and accurate information and helpful guidance.

STAY HEALTHY AND PHYSICALLY FIT

Another piece of advice I've shared with many young people and my employees is that it's important to stay physically fit and healthy. Take care of your body and your mind. You'll feel better about yourself and be able to do your job that much better.

You'll also have more energy and find it easier to maintain a positive attitude about everything. I've always practiced what I've preached by working out every weekday at the gym, eating healthily, never drinking, and giving up smoking many years ago.

ADVICE FOR SETTING GOALS

The difference between a job and a career is that a career is something you plan to pursue until you retire. A job has a short-term annotation. During your career, you may take on many different positions, but ideally, you want each job to represent some sort of career advancement.

A young person might hold several jobs before they discover what they want to pursue for their career. Once you've reached that point, it's a good strategy to understand the career path you want to take. Create clearly defined short- and long-term goals that will help you achieve your ultimate objectives.

A short-term goal when it comes to your career might be to earn a promotion and take one step up the proverbial corporate ladder by the end of the year. Your long-term goal, however, might be to become a senior vice president of a specific company, or to start your own business within the industry you're working in within the next five years.

Setting realistic goals for yourself can help you stay on track, look at the big picture, and understand what you need to do to keep your career moving forward. For each big goal you set, divide it up into a series of smaller, short-term goals that are more easily achievable. Next, determine what you need to accomplish to complete each of those smaller goals, and set deadlines for yourself to achieve each of them.

As you're figuring out how to achieve any goal, consider what skills, knowledge, and professional experience you still need to acquire. Then, develop a plan for acquiring the skills, knowledge and experience that's required.

Not only should you write down each of your short-term and long-term goals, keep a written log of your progress and upcoming deadlines as you work toward each objective. Knowing what you need to do and how you plan to do it will help keep you focused and motivated.

During the Civil Rights Movement, Alice West coined the phrase, "Keep your eyes on the prize." It was then incorporated into a song which became the anthem of this movement. And in 1963, the phrase was used in the Pete Seeger song, "We Shall Overcome." This is a long way of saying that you too should keep your eyes on the prize as you're working your way toward achieving your bigger, long-term goals. Focus on your career and what you want from it.

If you're someone who wants to work a 9:00am to 5:00pm job for the rest of your professional life, that's fine. But if you have bigger aspirations, you need a well-defined plan for achieving them. Understand that the more you want out of your career, the harder you'll need to work, and the more focused and motivated you'll need to be.

Based on my personal experiences, having plenty of money is a good thing. However, this should be a byproduct of achieving your career goals. You want to be proud of the work you do on an ongoing basis. Focus on doing superior work to stand out, as opposed to doing just average work that anyone with your job title and responsibilities can accomplish.

Money should not be your key motivator. Again, if you're going to invest so much of your life toward achieving something, do what you're truly passionate about. Once you find that, figure out how to make the most money you can, in the least amount of time.

If you don't like what you're doing, find something else. There are many different opportunities out there, and if you think outside of the box, you may be able to create your own opportunities. Whatever approach you take, don't keep pursuing something that makes you miserable or that you do not find rewarding.

Loving my career was a key factor in my own success. I've also seen this with countless other people who now run their own business or have earned the CEO title of a company.

YOUR CAREER PATH MIGHT INCLUDE BECOMING THE BOSS

The advice I offered just touches the surface of what you'll likely experience in the working world, but it will hopefully help jumpstart your career, so you can eventually achieve wonderful things.

That said, not everyone wants to become an entrepreneur, CEO, or the boss. If you do, in the next chapter I share my strategies and advice about how to become an amazing boss and do a good job managing employees. If this is not part of your career path, skip to Chapter 7, "Even with Ups and Downs, Don't Forget to Enjoy Life to Its Fullest."

6

How to Become an Amazing Boss and Manage Employees

"Success is liking yourself, liking what you do, and liking how you do it."

MAYA ANGELOU

WHETHER YOU take on a supervisory, managerial, or executive role while working for an employer, or choose to launch your own business and be the boss, you will take on a lot of extra responsibilities. How I personally handled these tasks over the years is what you'll read about in this chapter. My management styles and philosophies certainly evolved over the years, so I focus here on the information I believe is still relevant today.

Keeping this in mind, the type of business you choose to run, or the industry you wind up working in may require adapting some of these strategies or moving in a different direction altogether. It's my belief, however, that at least some of what you're about to read will be directly relevant to you and your career as a business leader or entrepreneur living and working in the first part of the 21st century.

If you work for someone else, you're likely not the final decision maker when it comes to bigger issues, but as the boss, everything falls onto your shoulders. As a boss, you need strong leadership skills. You also must understand everything about your business, the products/services it offers, and your industry.

Being a boss, entrepreneur, or business owner is much more than a collection of skills and experiences you put into your daily work. It's a lifestyle and mindset. Working hard for long hours each day, staying motivated, and being goal-oriented should all be part of your entrepreneurial mindset.

And one thing I cannot stress enough is the importance of having a reliable support system. For me, this always included my family, but during certain periods of my professional life, I also relied heavily on my business partner(s).

Also, I strongly advise against starting a business in an industry you know absolutely nothing about and have no experience working in. You need to understand your business, its products/services, and the industry you'll be a part of, starting from day one. You should also maintain realistic and achievable goals for yourself and your business venture. There's little to no room for magical thinking.

This knowledge will help you properly equip your business and hire the right employees. It will also make it easier to identify and reach prospects/clients. You need to know who your target customers/clients are, what their needs are, how to win them over, and then how to keep them loyal to your company over the long haul.

Meanwhile, if your business will be relying on suppliers, for example, do your research to pinpoint the best and most reliable companies to work with. This also means finding one that offers high-quality products/services, fair pricing, and that works well with its clients (including your business). You need to be able to trust your supplier(s) to always be able to get you what you need on time. Any delays can become very costly and cause you to lose your own clients/customers if you can't offer them what they want or need when they want or need it.

Ultimately, having just one really good supplier is not enough. Have two or even three backup suppliers lined up, so if you can't get what you need from one, you have a plan in place to get quickly and affordably what you need elsewhere. My philosophy has always been to buy the highest quality products and equipment made in the United States.

Whenever I needed to find a new supplier, I always found it by attending trade shows, or through a word-of-mouth referral from someone I knew and trusted. I never randomly selected a supplier out of the phonebook or later via a random Google search.

DO YOU HAVE WHAT IT TAKES TO BE THE BOSS?

Before you decide to start your own business, I recommend that you go out and talk to as many already well-established and successful business owners as you can. Preferably, these should be people who work in the same industry you plan to work in, but this isn't a requirement.

Ask these people what it really takes to be a successful entrepreneur or business leader from their perspective. Many people get caught up in the excitement and lure of being their own boss, but don't realize what taking on this responsibility really entails. Make sure you understand what you're getting into, the risks involved, and the personal sacrifices you'll likely need to make.

If you have the passion and desire to start a business, go for it. Don't let anything hold you back. Understand that you may need to try a handful of different things until you discover the right formula for the business and your management style. Yes, starting a business or being an entrepreneur can be a risky endeavor, but if you decide to give it a try, stick with it. Don't quit as soon as you're faced with your first problem or setback.

What sets business leaders apart from people who spend their career working for someone else comes down to one word—desire. It has to be something you really want to do. Once I learned how to be an elevator mechanic and developed those skills, I decided I wanted to learn the business part of it and become my own boss.

I discovered rather quickly that it's very hard to start a service business and earn a good living all by yourself. You must have people working for you. You might be able to charge $100 per hour for your own labor, but if you have five or more people working for you, and can charge $100 per hour for each of them, but you can keep $25 to $50 of that, the money adds up much faster.

As "the boss," I was never someone who just ordered people around like a dictator. You need your employees to like you and respect you. Instead of saying things like, "This is what I want you to do to make my company successful," say something like, "This is what we should do for us to be successful." Make it clear everyone is part of a team.

Anytime someone asks what I think it takes to run a business, I immediately say that you need to be available 24 hours a day, every day to deal with problems that arise. And it's a requirement to juggle many responsibilities at once. It's also an expectation that personal sacrifices are required, and you will have to make many important decisions that can impact a lot of people. If you're up to these tasks, go for it.

20 CORE SKILLS EVERY BUSINESS LEADER NEEDS

Over the years, I've had to expand my skillset to stay on top of my game as a business leader. Sometimes, this meant working on tactile skills like project management, while other times, it meant sharpening my emotional IQ.

Regardless of the type of business or industry you work in, I believe leadership positions require a core skillset that, in alphabetical order (not order of importance), includes:

1. Conflict Resolution Skills
2. Critical Thinking Skills
3. Decision-Making Skills
4. Delegation Skills
5. Emotional Intelligence
6. Interpersonal Skills
7. Listening Skills
8. Managerial Skills
9. Motivational Skills
10. Multitasking Capabilities
11. Negotiation Skills
12. Problem Solving Skills
13. Project Management Skills

14. Relationship Building Skills
15. Strategic Thinking Skills
16. Stress Management Skills
17. Team Management Skills
18. Technical Skills (Understanding Computers and Basic Technologies)
19. Time Management, Planning, and Organizational Skills
20. Written and Verbal Communication Skills

You also need to be able to adapt quickly, be open to change, be a risk taker, and have the ability to inspire others. Being self-aware, confident, courageous, empathetic, honest, trustworthy, respectful, resilient, friendly, creative, compassionate, and able to serve as a teacher and mentor are also potential requirements. I am not saying these things to scare or overwhelm you, but to help you develop realistic expectations about what you're getting yourself into.

It's your responsibility to create and maintain a positive and safe workplace and company culture. And all this is on top of being the visionary for your company. As you review this list, keep in mind that not all of these skills are taught at even the best business schools.

Some of these skills can only be acquired through hands-on and real-world experience, while others can be learned by reading books, taking online courses, and working with mentors, for example. All require practice to become proficient using them.

Looking back at my own career, I learned some of these skills from my parents and through my education. I learned many of these skills from working for other people in various jobs. My business partners and mentors taught me some of these skills over the years, and some I had to figure out on my own. Of course, over the years I also studied other successful business leaders, including others working in my industry.

One thing I've discovered over time is that knowledge comes from all around you. You simply need to stay open-minded, be willing to listen, and absorb the information that can help you achieve success. You never know where inspiration might come from, and the best inspirations can lead to new and innovative ideas.

LEARN WHEN TO SEEK HELP OR SUPPORT FROM OTHERS

Early in your management career, one lesson you also need to learn is that you do not know everything. Nobody does. Having self-awareness is essential. You need to know when to be honest with yourself, quickly identify when you don't know or understand something, and then actively seek out the information that's needed. This might mean doing research or seeking help or advice from others (including your employees).

There are times when seeking help from others makes strategic sense for the wellbeing of your business. Six of these instances include:

- When you're personally overwhelmed.
- Anytime you're unsure about how to proceed with something.
- If you're faced with a difficult conflict that needs a swift solution.
- If you could benefit from different perspectives when formulating a better solution to something.
- In situations where you do not have the knowledge or skillset to make well-informed decisions on your own.
- When facing legal, financial, safety, highly sensitive, or other situations that require specialized knowledge or skills.

In situations when I didn't know the answers, I sometimes used a trial-and-error approach, as I've mentioned earlier. I'd keep trying new things until I achieved the desired objective. This too is a strategy that can work, but not always.

Ultimately, the more of these skills you acquire and become good at using, the better off you'll be when it comes to dealing with the day-to-day challenges of running a business and managing employees. Part of your mindset as a business leader and entrepreneur should be to continuously learn new things and always be open to hearing other peoples' points of view.

Not all entrepreneurs have college or graduate-level education. Like me, you can still run your own business in many industries. I always made a point to try to learn from employees and people around me who were better educated. That included people I considered my mentors.

LEAD BY EXAMPLE

It's one thing to be the boss and tell your employees what to do, when to do it, how to do it, and how to act. But I found that if you lead by example, it's much easier to earn the respect of those working for you.

For example, being the first person to show up at the office each day, and then the last person to leave sets a strong precedent. It was one way I demonstrated my strong work ethic. It showed that if I could do it, so could they. If you expect employees to dress and act a certain way while at work, follow these guidelines yourself. Anytime you set expectations for others, make it clear (through your actions) that those expectations apply to you as well.

As the boss, I was always consistent and followed the same rules I'd expect my employees to follow. When necessary, I was accountable for my mistakes. I was also able to support my decisions with timely and accurate information. In addition, I tried to always communicate clearly with my employees, so they were never left wondering what I really meant when I said something.

Most importantly, there were countless times when I worked alongside my employees, both in the office and in the field. I never assigned other people tasks that I was not willing to do myself. Yet, I was careful not to micromanage my employees, unless they were doing something wrong. Over the years, I discovered that my employees would learn and try to replicate my positive attitude and work ethic simply by seeing it every day—even without me asking them to.

When you lead by example, it's easier to build trust and earn respect from your subordinates. I found it also builds loyalty and helps increase productivity. Anytime I made a promise, I did my absolute best to follow through on it.

Through my actions, I made clear that I supported my employees in every way possible. At the same time, I was not a pushover people could abuse. I was always fair, but strict when I needed to be. I knew that as the business's leader, I had to set the right impression and always maintain a level head.

Even if I was mad, I would bite my tongue and try to resolve whatever conflict that arose in a quiet, professional, and peaceful manner. I did this even when what was going on inside my head was very different. I always took the time to listen to the other person's grievance and figure out if maybe I was the one at fault. (Yes, like everyone else, I too have been known to make mistakes.)

Being able to look at problems from multiple perspectives is another skill I developed over time. I used it when managing people and dealing with difficult clients. Another thing I did is maintain a neat, clean, up-to-date office. For the people who worked in the office, I tried to keep the place well-lit and at a comfortable temperature, too.

If someone wanted to move their desk to be closer or further away from the heat or air conditioning, or desired a location that had better lighting, I always tried to accommodate those requests to keep everyone happy and productive.

My management style was always very flexible and fair. I tried to make it clear that if someone had a problem, they should come to me directly. Part of being a good boss, at least in my opinion, is being available to employees.

When someone needed to go home early once in a while or take a few days off to deal with a personal or family issue, I tried to accommodate their requests and be flexible. My goal was always to hire people I trusted. And if they've been with us for a long time and had demonstrated their loyalty in the past, I tended to be even more generous and flexible whenever possible.

BE ON THE LOOKOUT FOR NEW OPPORTUNITIES

First, get into a business that you really enjoy and that will be part of an industry that's growing. You really need to be passionate about your company's products and services. You should be happy and proud of what you're doing. Once you commit to starting a specific type of business in a specific industry, you're potentially making a very long-term commitment.

Whether you're first kicking around the idea of starting a new business, or you already run one, always be on the lookout for new opportunities. Keep your ear to the ground and stay informed with what's happening in your industry and in the world around you. Pay attention to what your competition is up to and become aware of up-and-coming trends that could lead to new or expanded revenue streams.

When I analyzed my competitors, I looked at what they were doing that I was not. If it made sense, I'd then try to replicate their success but do things even better. There was one guy many years ago who ran an elevator business, and I thought he was an absolute dummy. I didn't pay much attention to what his company was up to.

However, he eventually brought his two sons into the business, and then suddenly their business (my competitor) started doing very well and growing quickly. That's when I took notice and tried to figure out what they were doing right.

One way I discovered new opportunities was to attend lots of industry-oriented trade shows and gatherings. I spoke with lots of people and looked for ways I could work with other companies in my industry in a way that would allow all of us to become more successful. When it came to insuring my business, for example, it was by working with industry partners that we were able to get the best deals and coverages, especially when it came to worker's compensation insurance.

SOMETIMES, IT MAKES SENSE TO HAVE A BUSINESS PARTNER

Sometimes, opportunities will come knocking at your door, but most of the time, you need to go out and actively discover them. One strategy I used to make this easier was to have a business partner with whom I got along, trusted, and respected. He had the same overall vision for the company as me. Now, two people were working toward the same goals and seeking out the best potential opportunities.

My business partner during the earlier years at Embree Elevator did a good job at reigning me in when I wanted to take on something big that didn't make good business or financial sense. I did the same for him. We provided a good checks and balance system for each other, and that worked out favorably for the business as a whole. My business partner was someone I worked with at a previous company, so we started with mutual respect and a friendship. That was very helpful.

The advice I have for a business leader in search of a partner is to find someone who's well qualified and honest. This applies to his personal and professional life. If a potential business partner has already been through three marriages, that's a huge red flag. Also, if they tend to go to a bar every day after work to get drunk, or they gamble heavily on weekends, those habits too can easily become problematic for the business.

In other words, evaluate the whole person you're looking at to become a potential business partner. Do not just focus on their education, skills, and past professional accomplishments.

Once you choose a partner, make sure all of the financial and legal paperwork is done correctly, so everyone is well protected if the partnership does not work out, or one of the partners leaves the business (as a result of retirement, dissatisfaction, or death). This is an example of when having good lawyers and financial advisors comes into play.

CAN EMPLOYEES BECOME CLOSE FRIENDS? WHERE TO DRAW THE LINE

When it came to my business partners, we worked very well together on the job and always had each other's backs, but we never socialized outside of work. At the end of the workday, he'd go home to his family, and I'd go home to mine.

My management philosophy was much the same with my employees through the years. I was always friendly with them at work, and we all worked well as a team. But, outside of work, there was no socialization between me and them.

Anytime something happened at work that required everyone's attention, I'd gather everyone together and speak with them openly and honestly, like a trusted colleague. Again, I wanted to maintain two way trust and for everyone to maintain a sense of pride in the work they were doing.

On days when someone did a really good job, I always made a point to complement their work and offer plenty of encouragement. But outside of work, I had my own set of friends who were not associated with the business. Of course, this no socialization philosophy never applied to the relatives who were a valuable part of the business.

It was a normal occurrence, however, for groups of employees to go out to a bar after work or socialize among themselves. As long as it didn't interfere with their work, I had no problem with that.

FUNDING YOUR STARTUP BUSINESS VENTURE

I guess I was lucky because for each business that I started throughout my career, I was either able to finance it myself or was eligible to get loans from a bank. When I took over Embree Elevator with my business partner and wife, I used my savings, sold stock in another elevator company I owned, and sold my vacation property.

I believed that having financial skin in the game kept me focused on making the business as financially successful as possible, as quickly as possible. If you're going to take on investors, make sure you understand how much of your business (and control over your business) you'll be giving up by taking their money.

Consider working with investors, including relatives, that you know personally and who you trust and have had previous dealings with. I would try to find investors who would accept non-voting stock, as opposed to giving away a percentage of the company and decision making control related to it.

About 50 years ago, I had a friend who owned a successful computer company. He wanted to expand and took on several investors. One day, he was president of the company, but then he was suddenly voted out and lost his business. This guy took advice from the wrong people and gave away too much control and ownership of his business.

WAYS TO FIND, HIRE, AND MANAGE THE BEST EMPLOYEES

For some types of companies, finding employees is easy if you're willing to pay a fair wage and offer basic training for a job that does not require too much skill, a college education, or previous experience. But for higher level roles within a business, and when you need employees with technical skills, finding, hiring, and retaining the best employees is much more of an ongoing challenge.

Now that Embree Elevator has been around for so long, we have children of previous employees who are now grown up and working for us. We also have a great relationship with the union and can reach out to many people we know in the industry if we have an opening for a managerial, supervisory, or mechanic role that requires industry knowledge and specialized skills.

When we first started out, I sought out referrals from people in the industry whom I knew and trusted. In situations where we could not immediately pay the highest wages, I explained that if the new worker stuck with the business and helped it grow, I would be generous with their salary as soon as we could afford to pay more. Because the employees were taking a risk on the company, they tended to be more loyal since they had a financial interest in its future success.

It was always a balancing act to have the right number of employees, so we could keep overtime pay to a minimum. I think word got out quickly about how much our employees enjoyed working for us, and this made it easier to find others who anxiously wanted to join our team. This is still the case today.

I wanted to own a business that treated our employees fairly and provided a friendly, safe, and welcoming culture. I am proud we were able to accomplish this early on, and maintain the same strategy through the decades, which is why so many people have stayed with us over the years. I am truly proud of that and consider it to be one of my career's best accomplishments.

I often did special things for the employees, like buy them family-size turkeys for Thanksgiving and Christmas and provide free gym memberships to whomever wanted one. They really appreciated those informal and often unexpected extras.

On an ongoing basis, we always offered cookies, coffee, and muffins every morning in the office. Once we became a union shop, to keep everyone happy, I offered the same (union specified) pay to all union and non-union employees. Again, I wanted to be fair.

Of course, there were times when an employee would not live up to expectations. Instead of bringing them into my office for a reprimand, I'd first ask one of their co-workers or their supervisor to say something to them casually and unofficially. If things didn't improve, I'd talk to them directly, or turn things over to the union, but I tried to give employees the benefit of the doubt as much as possible.

One of the things I would not tolerate from employees, however, is if they started badmouthing the company publicly instead of coming to me first with their grievances. Not only did this offend me personally, but it also risked tarnishing the reputation of the business, which would impact all of the employees. I never understood why someone would try to bite off the hand that feeds them, so to speak.

From a management standpoint, I always discussed with employees what my expectations of them were for the job they filled. Back in the day, this was all done verbally. I would then pair up each new employee with someone who's been with us for years, so the new guys could learn the ropes. This way, they'd easily figure out the basics, like how they needed to put on a clean uniform each day, what time they needed to show up for work, and how to present themselves while on a job.

Teaming up the new guy with a veteran employee always proved to be the best on-the-job training. I did not create a formal written employee handbook or detailed job descriptions. These days, however, that's very important to do. It's necessary to make sure everyone is on the same page and understands what's expected of them.

Another management strategy I used was that when an employee deserved a promotion, I waited for them to ask for it. So, I knew they were invested and ready for more responsibility. I'd also pay attention to what the employee's coworkers had to say about them before I offered the promotion.

In my industry, when someone transferred from being a mechanic in the field to being a supervisor in the office, it changed their status with the union, so they had to consider those ramifications, too.

When it came to giving raises, I'd base it on each individual's performance, and how much they were earning for the company. It was based on what I believed that person could produce moving forward. I left some room for negotiation, but I never based the amount of a pay raise on a predetermined percentage.

Of course, there were situations when someone would ask for a raise but didn't deserve it at that particular time. When this occurred, I'd outline what they needed to accomplish to make themselves more valuable to the company. Also, if they asked for a specific amount for their raise, I'd typically offer them a percentage of the requested amount. I'd then explain that it was a test run. If they lived up to expectations, after a specific amount of time, I'd give them the full raise they requested. I did this all on a case-by-case basis.

As the boss, all of the decisions you make related to your employees need to be in the best interest of the company and its public reputation. In our business, most of our customers come to us through a positive word-of-mouth referral. If there is an employee preventing customers from giving us a stellar review and recommending us, that person is not working in the best interest of the company. As a result, they are probably unsuitable for us.

People don't understand how essential it is for any business to build and then maintain a positive reputation, especially in today's online world where there are sites dedicated to publishing company reviews written by customers, and an individual can reach thousands of people with a single social media post. Building and maintaining a company's reputation starts at the top, but depends on the hard work, loyalty, and dedication of all the company's employees.

KEEP UP WITH THE CHANGING TIMES

Back in the 1930s when I was born, and while growing up in what was the small town of Bedford, Massachusetts (where I still live today), things were very different than they are now. By default, like everyone else living at the time, I had to adapt to new ways of living and evolving new technologies.

Televisions were not yet in all American homes when I was a child. Indoor plumbing was first becoming common, and antibiotics (which we take for granted today) were still experimental. As a result, a small infection could become deadly. And in the southern United States, there was still segregation. Cars were a new thing that, at the time, only wealthy people owned. Of course, there was no internet, no computers, and no smartphones. If you wanted to cross the Atlantic Ocean, you did so by ship, not by airplane.

In my teenage years and as a young adult, I appreciated new technologies and the evolutions taking place in our society. I took advantage of them as a young entrepreneur. As an adult, when I ultimately started my own businesses, it became vitally important to stay informed about the latest technologies and determine how to best use them in my business.

Decades later, the need to stay informed, study technological innovations, adopt technology in constructive ways, and understand changes and trends happening in society are still necessities for today's business leaders and entrepreneurs. Today, for example, business leaders are struggling to figure out how artificial intelligence will impact their respective companies, their industry, and society as whole.

So, while technologies and trends change over time, the need to understand and leverage them when it's appropriate is still a sound business practice. I think it's also the most savvy and creative entrepreneurs who discover the most innovative ways to use the latest technologies. Those are the people who can stand out and achieve greater success.

I stated earlier that nobody likes change, and some people are afraid of it. However, part of having an entrepreneurial mindset is to embrace change and be able to adapt to it as needed. As a business leader, if your mind and practices are stuck in the past, your company will be left behind. So, if you don't fully understand the latest trends and technologies, hire people who do, so they can help you and your business stay current.

DON'T FORGET TO LIVE YOUR LIFE TO ITS FULLEST

Throughout this book, I've written extensively about how running your own business represents a tremendous commitment and requires many personal sacrifices. This is all very true. I also wrote about how important it is to maintain a work/life balance. This is also very true.

The term "work hard, play hard," however, applies and has been around for years. My work/life balance mainly evolved around my family, but over the years involved taking on many projects and participating in so many activities that I loved. It was my family and these pastimes that ultimately made my life amazing and allowed me to create so many fond memories that I can look back on today.

The next chapter focuses a bit more on the ways I enjoyed my life outside of work. Hopefully, it will provide you with ideas on how to achieve a similar objective doing things that you enjoy with people you care about.

7
Even with Ups and Downs, Don't Forget to Enjoy Life to Its Fullest

"All work and no play makes Jack a dull boy. All play and no work makes Jack a mere toy."

JAMES HOWELL (circa 1659)

I'VE LIVED a happy and blessed life, and it's still going strong. I had an incredible marriage. We raised amazing children, and we've lived in a really beautiful town. Throughout the decades, I've been able to work with and for so many genuinely nice people. It's been a great life, and I have very, very few regrets.

Sure, I always had long-term goals and dreams, but I also lived life day-by-day. If you're young, there's still plenty of time for you to achieve a similar life that's filled with prosperity, happiness, and love. But it's something you need to work hard for. It's not something that will simply be given to you.

I discovered a lot has to do with having priorities. Family, my health, and work always came first. Then, with whatever time was left, I spent pursuing other pastimes, which whenever possible involved working with my hands because this was something I enjoyed. If I didn't put effort into maintaining my health, I doubt I'd have lived this long.

When you manage to achieve your goals and dreams, congratulate yourself and be sure to take the time to appreciate it. Enjoy what you have, instead of being angry that you don't yet have certain things you want. But, if there is something you still want or need out of your life, figure out how you can get it, and then do the necessary work.

I've already discussed the necessity for a business leader—or anyone in the workforce—to maintain a positive work/life balance. Not only will this help you avoid burnout and enjoy more of what life has to offer, it'll also help you enrich the lives of your family and friends. This is because you'll be spending quality time with them.

As important as my work has always been to me, it is my family that's hands down the most important. Now, as the patriarch of my family, I have seen firsthand how spending quality time with my four kids, eight grandchildren, two step-great-grandchildren, and other family members has allowed me to maintain a close-knit and loving extended family.

Throughout my life, I have also found time to pursue personal interests outside work. These activities have included going to the gym on a regular basis; attending church and having family dinners on Sundays; being able to travel to exciting places around the world on vacations (during my adult years); and over the past twenty-five years or so, spending portions of the summer with my extended family in East Hampton.

At the same time, as you strive to do your very best at work, figure out what you enjoy doing when not on the job. Discover hobbies and pursue your passions. Determine what activities will allow you to clear your mind from the stresses of your career and simply enjoy yourself.

Whether you pursue golf, fishing, gardening, camping, knitting, rebuilding cars, travel, boating, or restoring an old home, it does not matter, as long as you enjoy it. And it's even better if you can share that hobby or passion with your loved ones and friends.

Playing an active role in my lifelong hometown of Bedford, Massachusetts has also been an enriching part of my personal life. It's the town I was born in. In fact, my family's presence in New England dates back to 1640.

My involvement in the community has included volunteering for more than 40 years at the First Church of Christ and St. Michael's Parish, serving on the board of the Bedford Grange for more than three decades, and being a part of the town's chapter of the Lion's Club. I have always appreciated the small town lifestyle and attitude.

Another highlight of my life involves restoring the 200-year-old home I currently live in within Bedford, which was a project my wife and I took on when we purchased the Elijah Stearns Mansion back in 1984. The 6,000-square-foot home is on the National Register of Historic Places.

My passion for safety in the elevator industry led me to volunteer my time for more than 20 years to the Massachusetts Board of Elevator Resolutions in the state's Department of Public Safety and helping to establish The Elevator Museum in 2012 with my son. It was my volunteer work in the elevator industry that allowed me to have an impact on elevator safety regulations throughout the United States and around the world.

For volunteering in my industry, I earned the Ellis Island Medal of Honor. I did not do this for the accolades, however. I did it as a way to make elevators safer for those who build, inspect, maintain, and repair them, and the billions of people around the world who ride in them every day.

Over the years, I had seen firsthand and heard about so many elevator-related accidents and deaths. I believed many of them might have been avoided with better safety protocols and more reliable equipment, so that was what I set out to achieve.

Plus, throughout my adult life, I've been involved in a wide range of philanthropic projects, including the founding of the Virginia Comley and James F. Comley Endowed Scholarship, which is part of the UMass Lowell Endowment. It directly supports first-generation college students.

I have always lived by the philosophy that it's important to genuinely be nice to people, and to help those who need it. If more people lived by this philosophy, I think the world could be a better place. Doing philanthropy work or donating to charity should not be something done for accolades or out of obligation.

Volunteer and philanthropy work should be done because it's something someone wants to do—because they feel good about it and enjoy it. I think people should help people, and the charitable causes they're passionate about or have an interest in, whatever they may be.

I have learned that how you spend your time outside of work is as important (if not much more important) in your life as what you accomplish throughout your career. Having strong family values is something I learned from my grandparents and parents and then have done my absolute best to pass on to the next generations.

Beyond being there for regular family dinners throughout the years (not just on holidays), I made a point to attend the important events as my children and grandchildren were growing up. This included everything from recitals and sports games to birthday parties, graduations, weddings, anniversary parties, births, and unfortunately, some funerals.

My goal was to be successful in business while having a personal life filled with love and activities I was passionate about. My hard work provided the financial resources to live the personal life I always dreamed about as a child.

So, when someone asks if I believe a lifetime of hard work in the elevator industry was worth it, I can unequivocally say yes. Not just because of the financial stability Embree Elevator continues to provide my family, but because that stability has allowed all of us to live comfortable lives and be able to pursue our passions outside of work.

As my children and then grandchildren were growing up, I wanted to provide absolutely everything they needed, from personal belongings and a comfortable home to a well-rounded education and the ability to experience the world outside of Bedford.

I've also wanted the financial resources to give back to my community and industry and be able to financially donate to charities that I believed in, such as my church, the Cancer Society, and the American Red Cross.

Again, these are values instilled in me by my parents, grandparents, and in-laws—who all also lived in Bedford, so they were around for much of my adult life, too. That is, until they passed away. There were decades when we all lived within a block from each other, so I also had cousins, aunts, and uncles all living close by (although most of them eventually moved out of town by the 1950s).

For all this, I am grateful that I had the personal, professional, family, and philanthropic opportunities that my decades of hard work at Embree Elevator has allowed for. I always loved my work, and I am now very proud of my legacy.

None of what I achieved could have been done without the love and support of my wife. I give her so much credit for our success. These days, it's my children and grandchildren who provide the most care and support to me, although I now have a cat named Loja. He is also very loyal. I've always had pets throughout my life, but this is the first time I've had a cat. I find his presence very soothing.

One thing I'd like people to learn by reading this book is that no man (or woman) is an island. It takes a family and community to live a happy and prosperous life, so never neglect your family or family-related obligations. These days, my kids keep finding new ways to keep my life interesting. It was Bonnie who urged me to write this book, for example, and it's been a fun and rewarding experience.

While I am still the owner and president of Embree Elevators, my involvement with the company is now minimal, since my daughter and son-in-law do such a marvelous job keeping it running successfully. Several times per month, however, I still go into the office. One of my grandsons just started working for the business, which I am very excited about.

BUILD FOR THE FUTURE WHILE PRESERVING THE PAST

Throughout my youth growing up in Bedford, my father and the rest of my family always admired the Elijah Stearns Mansion. It was one of the most elegant houses in the town. Much later in life, when the 200-year-old house went up for sale, I had the resources to purchase it. With my wife's blessing, I did. This was after my children were grown up and had moved out of the family home they all grew up in (also located in Bedford).

The house needed a lot of work, since very little maintenance had been done on it for more than 50 years. It sits on two acres of land. Our goal was to fix up the main house for ourselves and then have Carol build a separate, modern home for her family on the adjoining empty lot.

Because the Elijah Stearns Mansion needed so much work, we were able to buy it for a very good price. Of course, we then invested a lot of time and money in its restoration and preservation. I knew what the house looked like from when I was a child, so working on it became a labor of love for my wife and me. It was something we enjoyed together until she passed away.

Being good with tools and having always enjoyed restoring this, I took on the task of restoring the home back to its original glory. Meanwhile, my wife and I spent years amassing a collection of period-accurate artwork, furniture, and antiques to display within the original portion of the home.

Since it was built over 200 years ago, the house has undergone two major expansions. The first dates back 100 years, and the second one was more recent (but was added before we purchased it). Our goal was to fully restore the original portion of the home to its original glory, so when someone steps through the front door, they feel as if they've been transported back in time.

The Elijah Stearns Mansion is one of the community's few remaining old homes. Every day, it reminds me of what growing up in this town was like. Throughout the home there are lots of pictures of my family and me taken throughout the decades. Wherever I turn, it's filled with fond memories.

After many years of hard work, I believe my wife and I achieved our goal, although it's been an ongoing process that will probably never be fully finished. Until she passed, my wife and I lived mainly in the newer portion of the home, although we fully refurbished the original portion of the house, and the carriage house.

For a while, this is where Carol's adult children (my grandchildren) lived. We transformed this structure into a modern living space on the property yet kept the carriage house's original outside appearance.

And since my daughter and her husband live right next door in a home that was built about 15 years ago, she's spearheaded the massive task of designing and overseeing the maintenance of the beautiful landscaping that surrounds the connecting properties of all three homes and the detached multi-car garage.

I couldn't ask for a better life having my daughter, son-in-law, and some of my grandchildren living right next door. Meanwhile, my two sons and other daughter have moved out of Bedford to pursue their own lives but come back with their respective families often to visit. I also hear from most of them by phone almost daily, so they continue to be an important part of my life.

ACHIEVING SUCCESS REQUIRES YOU NEVER STOP LEARNING

During the more than 34,675 days I have been alive, I've learned and experienced so much. And most importantly, I've never gotten bored. I continue to be excited to wake up every morning and discover what the new day will bring.

One of the things I did when I first thought about writing this book was to sit down and summarize all of the most important lessons I've learned. I then encapsulated this information into 25 strategies that I firmly believe have helped me live a happy and prosperous personal and professional life.

In the next and final chapter of *The Ups and Downs of Business Ownership*, I have summarized these 25 success-related strategies that took me more than 95 years to discover. So, in the few minutes it takes you to read the book's final chapter, you can benefit from a lifetime's worth of knowledge that I sincerely hope everyone reading this finds useful.

This is all information I believe can be beneficial to anyone, of any age, no matter at what stage you are in your life, or what your career goals and dreams entail. It'll also be information that my fellow entrepreneurs, and up-and-coming business leaders and business owners can benefit from in their own journeys.

8
25 Philosophies that Helped Make Me Successful

"You don't have to see the whole staircase, just take the first step."

MARTIN LUTHER KING, JR.

DURING MUCH of my professional life, I did a lot of experimenting with various business strategies. I was always open to trying new things but was ready to adapt or pivot when things didn't go as planned. I often took a trial- and-error approach to problem solving, especially early in my career when the stakes were not as high.

These days, when it comes to making important business decisions, it's important to have a plan. Thanks to the internet, we have access to more information than ever before, and it's essential to use timely and accurate data to help reduce risks, understand your business, learn about your customers/clients, get to know your competition, and discover up-and-coming trends in the marketplace that could impact your bottom line.

While it's impossible to know with total certainty what the future will hold, you can't hold back in the business world. Generating creative ideas, building relationships, gathering the best possible team, having a reliable support system, properly managing your company's finances, and maintaining a clear picture of what you're trying to accomplish are all equally important.

Based on my experience, there are no shortcuts or cookie cutter solutions. Success requires hard work, commitment, and having realistic goals. Throughout this book, I've shared some of my career and personal achievements and discussed how they happened. I also described some of my biggest mistakes, how I overcame them, and what I learned from those experiences.

My professional life has involved working for and then owning service businesses in the elevator industry, but the core lessons I've learned can be applied to almost any type of business, in any industry. Before I finish writing this book and return to the joys of semi-retirement, I've summarized 25 of the most important evergreen business strategies I've learned that, throughout the decades, helped me achieve success.

One thing that definitely needs to be highlighted in this chapter is the importance of gratitude in your everyday life. No matter what you have, what you've achieved, or what situations you're facing, be grateful for it all, and for what you have the potential to do next. Focus on the good in life—both big and small. There will always be people who are less fortunate than you, and people who have more possessions, more money, and who are more successful. No matter what you do, you cannot change this.

Instead of comparing yourself and what you have with other people, focus on yourself, your health, your well-being, what you've already acquired, and all of your accomplishments thus far. Being grateful is a mindset you can control, as much as it is an emotion. And being grateful is a lot healthier and easier than being upset or jealous if you instead focus on the negatives, such as what you do not have, or what you have not yet achieved.

I have learned to appreciate what I have, and to never take anything for granted, whether it's my health, family, financial prosperity, my company, my community, church, my cat, or anything else that's a part of my life. These are all gifts, not a birthright. You never know when things could change for the better or worse. When it comes to happiness, focus on the present. As I have gotten older, I've become more grateful for my present, my good health, my past, and what's to come in my future.

For me, being grateful for my health means that every day, I can wake up and enjoy my day. At my age, I am still mentally lucid, physically mobile, and continue to be a part of family and work-related events. And I still have my memories. I believe that the exercise and health-related activities I engaged in throughout my life - mixed with good family genes and a bit of luck—has allowed for this. But, I also know things could change at any time, so I am grateful for each day.

There are four parts of gratitude—giving attention to what you're grateful for, acknowledging and giving value to it, appreciating it, and taking action in regard to it through your attitude, words, thoughts, or actions.

Being grateful does not mean being content, however. Once you know what you want to achieve during your life—personally or professionally—figure out what you need to do to make that happen. Then devote your time, energy, and resources to achieving your goals by adopting a well-thought-out and organized approach.

Understand that whatever you set out to achieve, it will take focus, hard work, dedication, and commitment. And yes, you will experience ups and downs along the way. That's part of life.

MY BEST AND MOST IMPORTANT ADVICE

Becoming an entrepreneur, business leader, or business owner can be scary. It's certainly a more difficult path to follow, compared to working for someone else and being an employee throughout your entire career. Once you decide this is something you want to pursue, simply take the first steps, put your whole heart into it, and just go for it.

As you move forward in the business world, wherever it takes you, keep these 25 strategies and philosophies in mind. Not all will apply to you at any given moment, but they could give you an edge and help you set yourself and your business apart in a positive way.

Listed here in no particular order, these strategies and philosophies could also help you navigate through difficult times, keep yourself motivated, and avoid mistakes that could potentially be detrimental to your business and personal success:

UNDERSTAND YOUR INDUSTRY

Much of what I learned about the elevator industry occurred on the job and by attending meetings and industry trade shows. It's important to learn everything you can about all aspects of your industry, starting as soon as you choose to enter into it.

This is most important if you plan on running your own business. Today, there's so much information you can acquire from the internet, but the way I did it was to learn from as many people in the industry as I could speak with in-person or by phone. Back then, even competitors tended to share advice and information freely. I believe networking is still extremely important, although these days it's something people often do online, using LinkedIn, for example.

In addition to having open conversations with people you know who are established and knowledgeable about your industry, I recommend also reading industry-related news, attending trade shows, and gathering as much timely and accurate data as you can from the internet and other sources.

While you want to understand the big picture, in terms of what your industry is all about, five things you need to keep tabs on that relate to your industry include:

- The size and strength of the industry as a whole, and how it's fairing in the current economy.
- Who the key players are (your competitors), what market share they hold, and why they're successful.
- How your business fits into the industry, and what it does differently from its competition that gives it an edge.
- What up-and-coming trends are on the horizon that could impact your business. This includes economic trends, and changes in the needs and demands of your customers/clients.
- How technology is impacting your industry. Learn ways you can use new technologies to stay ahead of your competition, save money, streamline certain business practices, and help your business operate more efficiently.

START SMALL, BUT PLAN TO EXPAND IF AND WHEN IT'S NEEDED

I have always taken a very conservative approach when it comes to growing my business. Early on, I determined what my company's niche in the industry would be, what geographic region it would cover, and how to best allocate our employees to offer the best possible services to our clients without being overstaffed or understaffed.

I've always sought out new opportunities that fit well with my company's overall objectives. If we chose to buy new equipment, hire more employees, slightly expand the area we serviced, or broaden the services we offered, we usually took small steps, and made intelligent decisions that required the least amount of risk possible.

I never wanted to be too reliant on bank loans to keep the business afloat. There were certainly times when we were offered really big jobs, but in my opinion, taking them on required too much risk, or having to commit too much money. I developed a successful way to manage my business and understand that sudden growth could jeopardize my ability to oversee everything, properly manage my employees, and offer personalized service to our clients.

So, anytime we decided to expand, the opportunity had to make sense. I had to know we'd be able to manage the growth, that the demand for our services would be there over the long-term, and any changes would not be too taxing on the company's resources.

I stayed away from opportunities that offered quick profit potential, but tremendous risk. I always preferred a slow and steady approach to my company's growth. My business decisions were never motivated by greed. Throughout the life of the business, I certainly wanted it to grow, but I also knew there was a certain plateau we should reach, and that's what I aimed for.

My concern was that if we grew too fast, we'd have to take on new employees, which meant needing additional supervisors. That required a larger office staff to manage everyone. And if too much growth happened too fast, we would not have time to properly train everyone or be able to maintain the same high level of service we offered to our clients. I never wanted to compromise that level of personalized service.

Also, because Embree Elevator was a family business, I knew that the decisions I made impacted the company and its employees, and the financial stability of my immediate family and the relatives that were involved with the business. I think that responsibility made me more cautious.

One tremendous difference between running a small or medium-size business or a family business—compared to a large corporation—is that the corporations are typically focused on generating the highest quarterly profits possible. As a medium-size business operator, I was always focused more on long-term success.

And because I was running a family business, I defined long-term as keeping the company profitable so it could be taken over by my children, and then my grandchildren, and so on. In other words, I was never willing to risk long-term success to make a quick buck or compromise my own business ethics.

To successfully implement a conservative, slow and steady growth strategy, consider the following steps:

- Build strong and long-lasting customer/client relationships with a focus on in-person communication.
- Continue to improve and refine your core product/service offerings based on customer/client feedback. When necessary, focus on small, incremental improvements that can give your business a competitive advantage.
- Be responsible with your company's money by not overextending it with too much debt or risky expansion. When it makes good financial sense, use profits to upgrade equipment and provide enhanced training to employees. I also believe in maintaining a cash reserve that can be used in emergencies, or for funding growth.
- Focus on operational efficiency. Try to reduce waste, improve profit margins, and take advantage of technology when possible to streamline systems like inventory management or scheduling.
- Be aware of industry trends, changes in customer/client behavior, and emerging technologies. Be ready to pivot and adapt wisely using timely and accurate information to make well-educated decisions that are not rushed.

DETERMINE WHAT SETS YOU AND YOUR BUSINESS APART FROM THE COMPETITION

I always took the time and got to know all my customers. I understood their short- and long-term needs, so I was able to cater what we offered specifically to each of them. For Embree Elevator, it was this personalized, consistently high-quality, reliable service that set us apart.

Whenever I sat down with a client, whether it was in their office or over lunch, I would ask them straight up if they were happy with our service and what we could do to improve it. I sought out honest feedback about the company, our services, and our employees. Much of our success comes down to building relationships. I believe this too is what continues to set us apart.

To this day, our clients know we are there for them 24/7 to maintain and repair their elevators. They understand we have highly qualified people working for us, and we never make compromises when it comes to the quality of the parts we use or the quality of service we provide.

Once you figure out what sets your business apart, make it a part of your company culture, and make maintaining that uniqueness part of your long-term objective. Focus on developing a strong reputation, and then consistently living up to it.

There are many ways a business can differentiate itself from its competitors:

- Offer a product or service that's unique in the marketplace, or that offers a stand-out customer experience.
- Provide exceptional customer service. Develop long-term relationships with your customers/clients in a way that builds trust and loyalty.
- Focus on niche markets. For example, while several of our biggest competitors catered to clients in the Boston area, we focused on areas outside of the city. If you're selling a product, consider offering something that caters to the needs of a very specific audience that you're able to reach affordably through marketing and advertising.
- Find ways to improve the products or services your company

offers. When possible, reinvent your offerings in a way that appeals to your customers/clients, but that's more forward-thinking than what your competitors offer.

- Focus on your company's unique brand and story. Promote your mission-driven values and the positive social impact your business offers. At Embree Elevator, our story is that we are an independent family business that provides superior services 24/7. We built our reputation based on honesty, promoting safety, and by offering reliability without price gouging our clients. This allows us to maintain a very favorable industry-wide reputation that results in the majority of our new clients coming from positive word-of-mouth referrals. When running a service business, I believe this is more beneficial and cost effective than many forms of traditional advertising.

"MADE IN THE USA" IS MORE THAN A MARKETING CATCHPHRASE

As a child, I did not travel abroad. My first opportunity to leave the country happened while I was in the Navy. Then, as I became successful as a businessperson, I was able to travel to many places around the world. Being able to travel provided exposure to new cultures. It also taught me there's no other place I'd rather live and work than in the United States of America.

As a businessperson, I have always been a firm believer in using American-made parts and supplies. They typically offer better quality and are more reliable. They're also easier to obtain. As an American business leader, I have always felt it was better to support my own country in whatever ways I could.

It was often the case that I could purchase parts and supplies overseas for less money, which would potentially increase my company's short-term profits. However, I chose to stay loyal to my patriotic beliefs.

Again, I was never greedy as a businessman. I'd rather use better-made parts and supplies that were reliable, and that I could easily get my hands on, even if it cost me more money and slightly cut into my short-term profit margin.

Most of our clients maintained long-term maintenance and repair contracts with us. So, over the long-term, using better quality equipment and parts has saved us money. My team could spend fewer hours maintaining our clients' elevators and have to do fewer repairs that were otherwise covered by a maintenance and repair contract.

I believe there are at least five compelling reasons why American businesses should support the "Made in USA" philosophy, including:

- It supports other U.S. businesses and our country's economy.
- It lowers a company's reliance on foreign suppliers, and allows for faster delivery times, plus better inventory control.
- U.S. manufacturing often offers enhanced labor, safety, and environmental regulations, which results in higher-quality products made using ethical production practices.
- It's environmentally responsible. By acquiring goods that are made within the U.S., this reduces emissions resulting from international shipping. Plus, U.S. factories operate under stricter environmental regulations than what you'd find in many other countries.
- When a business like mine can say its parts and supplies are made in America, this promotes patriotism in a way that many of our clients appreciate.

FOCUS ON THE SAFETY OF YOUR EMPLOYEES, CUSTOMERS, AND THE GENERAL PUBLIC

Whether you're providing products or services, safety is very important. I have dedicated my professional life to improving and expanding upon elevator safety procedures so that they're safer to work on, and safer for those riding them. When working with the Elevator Safety Board and helping the Federal regulations board, my objective was always to have elevators inspected more frequently than the current mandates called for.

These days, many companies pay less attention to the quality of their products and services, and I believe that's a mistake since this can directly impact safety. Even if it cuts into profits, I believe it's a company's responsibility to be as proactive as possible when it comes to safety—for the people providing their services or making the products, and for those relying on the services and using the products.

To ensure that employee, customer, and general public safety remains a priority at your business, here are five strategies that can help:

- Establish and clearly document safety protocols outlining workplace safety procedures, emergency procedures, and ways to keep customers, clients, and the general public safe when it comes to relying on your company's products and services.
- Provide safety training to all employees. This training should cater to their specific job and focus on everything from handling equipment to protecting the company against cybersecurity threats. The training should also cover how individual employees can help keep customers and the public safe through customer service-related interactions and outreach.
- Maintain a clean and safe workplace. If you're operating a service-oriented business, this should extend to job sites. Work areas should be kept clean, well lit, and free from any hazards. Make sure employees are aware of sanitation protocols, and how they're responsible to help keep their work environment as safe as possible. Of course, for a retail store, all aspects of the location should be kept safe for all customers and employees.
- Encourage employees to call out unsafe working conditions without fear of retaliation. This could include a way to address safety concerns anonymously. Remember that a safe work environment extends beyond physical safety. You want to foster a tolerant company culture that makes all employees feel safe and part of the team, regardless of their gender, sexual orientation, religion, age, or race, for example.
- Ensure that your employees have access to the most up-to-date and safest equipment. What this requires will vary based on the type of company you're running, but this must be addressed properly.

BUILD STRONG AND LASTING RELATIONSHIPS

Throughout my career, I have always focused on building long-lasting and honest relationships with my company's clients. This is one of the core reasons why I believe Embree Elevator became successful and has been able to last so long in the industry. These positive relationships help to boost the company's reputation.

By demonstrating our dedication, focus on quality, and reliability, anytime we needed to raise our rates, this was much easier for our clients to accept. They continue to believe we provide excellent value based on what we were charging.

Between the ever-increasing cost of parts and supplies, and the union salary requirements, there were times when our rate increases had to be higher than I would have liked. Since I was always transparent and honest, our clients knew that if we raised our rates, it was out of necessity, not greed.

Another instance where having strong relationships with clients occurs is when someone we have worked with for years changes jobs and begins managing different buildings. We're often able to keep the old client but bring in the new client since the person who is now working for that company already has a relationship with us. This is one of the ways we continue to generate a lot of new business. It all comes down to the quality of our relationships.

Having a relationship based on trust is also something a business owner should strive to attain with employees, too. Be open minded and listen to grievances and always provide positive feedback and praise when it's been earned. This leads to greater loyalty and better employee retention.

As a boss, I've learned that listening to employees' concerns is an essential part of my job. Sometimes people just need to be heard—getting something off their chest can make a real difference in how they feel and perform. When I take the time to listen, it not only helps the employee feel supported, but it also gives me insight into what's happening within the team. Even when a situation doesn't call for immediate action, I know that offering an open ear builds trust and reinforces that this is a workplace where communication and respect matter. I was always tolerant of peoples' quirky behaviors and attitudes if they proved to be hard working, reliable, and highly skilled employees.

Of course, there are times when even a long-lasting relationship comes to an end. Anytime this occurs, I have always listened to the other party and did whatever I could to part in a positive way, without burning any bridges. As a result, those people sometimes came back to us as a client later or referred us to other potential clients. This strategy also applies to employees.

When it comes to building strong and lasting relationships with customers and clients, consider implementing these strategies:

- Focus on delivering consistently high-quality service.
- Openly and honestly communicate with your customers/clients proactively and personally. Face-to-face meetings are ideal, while telephone calls can also do the trick. Emails and text messages are great for quick check-ins but are not suitable for building and maintaining strong customer/client relationships.
- Demonstrate your appreciation for your customers/clients. This can include anything from sending thank you notes to providing gifts, extra perks, or exclusive offers. Figure out what works best for your business.
- Ask for and pay attention to customer/client feedback. When it makes sense, act on that feedback promptly, so the customers/clients feel heard. Demonstrate your commitment to making improvements or fixing problems quickly, when necessary.
- Consider your customers/clients as long-term partners that are responsible for the success of your business. Make sure you're addressing their unique needs by providing the resources, education, and support they require.

GIVE BACK TO YOUR INDUSTRY AND COMMUNITY

This too was a philosophy that I pursued throughout my adult life from both a personal and professional standpoint. I outlined much of this volunteer work in the previous chapter. Over the years, I was involved in many different activities that helped my industry and community, but I was careful to ensure these added responsibilities had little impact on my work/life balance.

My rationale for being so active when it came to giving back was a result of being grateful for everything I had in life. And by joining the Navy, I was doing my patriotic duty for my country during the Korean War. I had many older uncles and cousins who served during World War II, so I was brought up learning about patriotism from my extended family members.

My time in the military taught me a lot. I worked hard and made my way up the ranks rather quickly. I eventually had people working under me, which is how I started to develop my people management skills. I also learned to get along with people who had different life experiences from me.

These turned out to be two very valuable skills that I wound up using throughout my professional life after my time in the Navy. So, while I was giving back to my country, my time in the military wound up being beneficial to my career. This was also where my belief in supporting the "Made in the USA" philosophy came from.

As a boss, I would always give preferential hiring treatment to people who served in the military. I knew they were responsible and respectful to management. To some degree this is also true of people who are part of a union. Union members get proper training, so I knew they were coming into the job being qualified to do it.

There are countless ways a business of any size can give back to its industry and community, some of which do not require a large financial investment or significant resources. Consider some of these strategies:

- Offer internships and apprenticeships through high schools, colleges, and trade schools, based on appropriateness. Develop ways your business' leaders can serve as mentors to young or up-and-coming professionals.
- Have your business support other local businesses and suppliers.
- Encourage employees to participate in volunteerism and reward them for their efforts. And when financially possible, have your company donate to charities that align with its values.
- Participate in industry-oriented events, workshops, and gatherings that promote learning and collaboration (and that benefit all participants, including competitors).

- Advocate for industry-wide standards when it comes to fair labor, environmental protection, and safety, for example. In my professional life, I volunteered thousands of hours to promote safety protocols and guidelines in the elevator industry. Not only did this help my business, but it also helps the industry, and the general public. It's had a lasting impact.

FOCUS ON THE HAPPINESS OF YOUR EMPLOYEES

As the boss, I tried to teach by example. So, when I was at the office, I'd bring my sense of humor and work ethic. While on the job, I would socialize with my employees and do my very best to maintain a positive, clean, and safe work environment.

I also listened to what my employees had to say, and made everyone feel like they were part of a team. By creating a positive work environment, I was able to keep my employees happy and focused. I believe my employees really appreciated me appreciating them.

Ensuring your employees are happy builds loyalty and can enhance productivity. It also creates a better workplace for everyone. As an employer, some of the strategies you can use to promote employee happiness include:

- Foster a positive and inclusive culture. You want your employees to feel safe, valued, and motivated.
- Support a work/life balance. Allow for some flexibility in scheduling and take steps to help avoid employee burnout. You can also consider allowing for a hybrid work situation, where employees can work from home several days per week, if the type of business you operate can allow for this. Plus, you can encourage employees to take the time off they're entitled to. Don't expect employees to be available outside of their traditional work schedule unless this is planned for in advance and part of an employee's job description.
- Encourage an open line of communication between management and employees. Make people feel heard, and that their ideas, opinions, and grievances matter.

- Provide ways for your employees to move their career forward by offering optional training opportunities, mentorships, and a clear path for promotion and skill building.
- Celebrate your employees' accomplishments and good work. This can be done in many ways, such as through shout-outs, bonuses, extra perks, or a simple thank you when someone goes above and beyond or demonstrates exemplary work.

BE A MENTOR TO OTHERS, AND PUT CAREFUL THOUGHT INTO CHOOSING YOUR OWN MENTORS

I have always had mentors myself—most were people in the elevator industry who were already successful and well established. I chose people who I wanted to model my career after. I then tried to serve as a mentor to my new employees; I also encouraged the new people to team up with the more experienced ones.

Being a mentor to others fosters a pay-it-forward mentality that can be beneficial to everyone. Mentees can benefit from mentors when it comes to inspiration and professional growth, while mentors can leave a lasting legacy and positively impact the careers of other people following in their footsteps.

Whether as a business leader you're serving as a mentor, or you seek guidance from a mentor, here are five potential benefits of mentorships:

- Promote learning, on-the-job training, and career growth opportunities.
- Provide guidance and support, plus help individuals overcome personal or professional setbacks.
- Expand networking opportunities within your company or industry.
- Boost confidence and motivation.
- Empower personal and professional growth by being able to follow in the footsteps of someone who's admired.

UNDERSTAND YOU CAN NEVER CONTROL EVERYTHING

This was a lesson I learned the day I started my first business. This is why I always surrounded myself with people who could help me. This included my wife and business partners, and the people I hired to be supervisors.

I chose to have business partners because I wanted people I could trust by my side. A business partner was there to help me make important decisions, be there when I could not, and could share some of the responsibilities and burden that comes with being the boss.

For me, when I faced a situation I didn't have control over, the first thing I did was grab a cup of coffee, sit down, and consider the situation carefully. I'd think about what I could do and consider each situation from several different perspectives. Having a business partner available to help me in these situations was usually very helpful.

My last business partner who helped me take over and initially run Embree Elevator (and who was not a family member) was someone I got along with really well. We trusted each other and rarely disagreed on how to proceed once we sat down to discuss things. And when the two of us could not come up with a solution, we'd seek out help from other knowledgeable people.

Even as a business owner and its CEO, you can never control everything. The sooner you come to terms with this fact, the better. Here are five strategies, however, that can help you maintain as much control as possible over your business:

- Set clear goals and objectives for your business, so you and everyone working for you knows what they're striving to achieve.
- Monitor the performance of your business and its employees. Pay attention to how things get done, revenue, customer retention, employee engagement, and operational efficiency. When necessary, find ways to improve things to keep everything running smoothly. At the same time, keep your business financially healthy by budgeting wisely, managing debt, and having a cash/credit reserve on hand if it's needed.
- Transform your employees into a loyal, hardworking team. Hire managers and supervisors that understand your business

operations and philosophies, so they are consistent when dealing with employees and customers/clients.

- When necessary, be proactive and ready to adapt to market shifts, evolving trends, and other challenges that arise.
- Learn how to delegate. Make sure you can trust the reliability and proficiency of the people you delegate important tasks to.

LEARN SOMETHING NEW EVERY DAY

You can start your career being smart, but if you don't continue the learning process throughout your lifetime, you will get stuck in the past and become kind of stagnant. I was always striving to learn new things, expand my skillset, and stay current. I mainly learned through life experiences and the people around me.

As a business leader or entrepreneur, you're going to be busy. However, I have lived by following the philosophy that I need to learn something new every day. This has helped me round out my education, stay informed, and become a better business leader.

Here are five strategies to help you learn something new every day:

- Read books, trade journals, newspapers, newsletters, web pages, and other publications that are business-related or industry-specific.
- Listen to podcasts or audiobooks. This is something you can do while driving, walking your dog, or while running on the treadmill, for example.
- Engage with people and strike up meaningful conversations that go beyond the current day's weather forecast.
- Ask questions and seek answers from people in the know. Also, take time to reflect and learn from your own experiences.
- Brainstorm new ways to approach things and try them. Try small experiments and learn from the results. And if you take a trial-and-error approach to problem solving, be ready to try something different if your approach fails but use that experience as your lesson of the day.

MAINTAIN A SENSE OF HUMOR

As the boss, I knew I needed to set the tone at the office. By nature, I have an upbeat personality and have always had a good sense of humor. I enjoy telling jokes. I carried these personal traits into my professional life, and they have served me well.

Business success isn't a joke, but you can maintain a good sense of humor as you pursue your success and interact with the people you encounter every day. Having a good sense of humor does not mean telling jokes in inappropriate situations or using humor to insult someone in any way.

When used properly, having a good sense of humor at work can help you:

- Build stronger relationships faster.
- Ease stress during tense situations.
- Help yourself and others boost their creativity and solve problems faster.
- Enhance communication and keep other peoples' attention. This can work well in meetings or during negotiations to lighten the mood. You can also use your sense of humor in-person, on the phone, during video calls, and in emails, and as part of your company's marketing/advertising (when it's appropriate).
- Establish a positive workplace culture and create a more collaborative environment.

STAY CURRENT IN A FAST-CHANGING WORLD

In 1597, Sir Francis Bacon coined the phrase, "Knowledge is power." As a business leader, you need to arm yourself with information that's relevant to your company's success. These days, there are so many ways to collect information. The trick is to be able to gather accurate and current information, process it, and use it to your advantage—without getting caught up in information overload. Keeping up with the times is important.

In my opinion, this strategy is directly related to learning something new every day. It's about obtaining and using information to your advantage.

Five ways to stay current include:

- Pursue lifelong learning. Keep your own skillset up-to-date with the latest business practices. Stay current on local, national, and global market demands and changes. And pay attention to what's happening within your own industry.
- Engage in networking within your industry. If possible, do this in-person by attending tradeshows, meetings, and workshops.
- Be prepared to adapt your leadership style and decision making strategies to accommodate new realities and changes in society.
- Conduct regularly scheduled strategic reviews within your company. Make sure everything that's being done aligns with market realities.
- Take advantage of the latest technologies, online-based tools, and even artificial intelligence (when appropriate) to handle things like market analysis, assist with automation or streamlining processes, and developing better customer insights. Being able to efficiently collect relevant data that's timely and accurate can help you make better decisions faster, so your business can stay competitive.

FORMAL EDUCATION CAN HELP, BUT IT'S NOT ALWAYS A REQUIREMENT

I am a firm believer in people having a well-rounded education. Based on the career path someone chooses to follow, earning a college degree or pursuing a higher level of formal education may not be necessary. But if you plan to pursue a specific trade, graduating from a trade school may be a prerequisite.

One of the ways I got my business, electrician, and elevator mechanic education was to spend several years working for other companies. I learned how to do the on-site work, but I also took the time to learn how a company operates. School can provide book smarts, but there's no better way to become educated than obtaining hands-on, real-world experience doing whatever it is you want to pursue for your career.

Five reasons to continue your education beyond high school include:

- To build a strong foundation for yourself, and discover more opportunities that are available, that you might not have otherwise learned about or considered.
- Education offers structure and teaches you how to learn on your own. This is a skillset that will last a lifetime. Based on my experience, formal education teaches you facts and makes you book smart, but real-world experience teaches you the skills needed for success in whatever career path you take.
- Pursuing an education allows someone to expand their professional network.
- Having a diploma demonstrates credibility and knowledge, although in my opinion, someone's performance and accomplishments in the real world can be more important than a diploma (that means someone has book smarts and can pass a series of written tests).
- Having a better education opens more doors, especially in today's competitive job market.

PRESERVE THE PAST WHILE BUILDING TOWARD A SUCCESSFUL FUTURE

No matter what you set out to do, create a plan. Put that plan in writing, so you can refer back to it often. The way I wound up preserving the past while building toward the future were twofold. I worked with my son to found The Elevator Museum, so people working in my industry could learn more about its past.

In my personal life, I purchased and restored my 200-year-old home, called the Elijah Stearns Mansion, in Bedford, Massachusetts. It's on the National Register of Historic Places. I love to keep busy—at work and at home. This is one reason why taking on the restoration project of my home was such a fun and rewarding challenge for me.

I have also been a fan of restoring old cars. At work, I got the most pleasure out of repairing old elevators. I enjoy taking old things and bringing them back to their former glory, especially when it involves working with my hands.

Here are five ways you too can help to preserve the past while focusing on the future as a business owner:

- Honor your brand's heritage by maintaining core values and continuing to use visual elements, such as a company's original logo or tagline. At the same time, you can update marketing content, product packaging, and put emphasis on digital marketing strategies.
- Create an accessible archive of institutional knowledge while training your staff to use the latest technologies and equipment.
- Consider retaining architectural features and design elements in your office or retail store in a way that reflects your company's history but upgrade its infrastructure to keep up with modern times.
- Continue offering legacy products or services, but ones that are redesigned to meet the needs of today's customers/clients.
- Maintain and expand your company's roots in its community, while finding new and innovative ways to expand support for local causes and events.

DON'T BE AFRAID TO TURN DOWN BUSINESS WHEN NECESSARY

If your team is already working at capacity, but you're not ready to hire new people, don't take on additional work you don't have the resources to handle. If you can do some internal reorganization to enhance productivity, that's a good solution. But decide to grow based on logistics and capabilities, not financial greed.

Spreading your team too thin could jeopardize the quality of work being offered, which could lead to dissatisfied clients. It's a balancing act.

If a potential client wanted us to install a make and model of elevator that we had no experience working with, and if it was just for that one potential client, I would pass them on to a competitor who already had expertise with that equipment. I did not want our people spending valuable time learning to use that new equipment if it was only for one client. Plus, not having expertise using that equipment could result in us doing inferior work.

But, if having our team develop an expertise working with that equipment meant we could bring in a bunch of new business, or I noticed a trend that our existing clients were moving to that make and model of elevator, I would take on the new business and get our team to develop the expertise needed to work with it and cater to the clients' needs.

When making the decision to potentially turn down new business, consider the following:

- Make sure you're sticking with your company's core mission, and that you're not over extending outside your area of expertise or specific niche.
- Pay attention to your capacity limits. Avoid overextending your employees, resources, or finances.
- Determine if the new business will disrupt your company's finances or compromise profitability in both the short and long term.
- Trust your instincts when necessary. Try to avoid taking on customers/clients that will be difficult to deal with, slow to pay, or that will require too much effort to properly manage.
- Just because your business is not ready to take on new business right away doesn't mean it never will be. Try to keep the opportunity available for the future when circumstances may change. Or use the opportunity to build an alliance or goodwill with a competitor by passing the potential customer/client over to them (if the competitor is better equipped to handle it).

GENERATE AND TEST NEW IDEAS

I have always been open to trying something new or different, especially if I thought it would benefit the company. Sticking with the same thing for too long gets stale and boring. By generating and adopting new ideas, it kept things interesting for me, and helped me stay motivated, even after many decades on the job.

When I decided to implement a new idea, I always paid attention to and monitored the outcome. I was ready to tweak the idea or, if necessary, scrap it altogether and try something else. Sure, there was some risk involved with this strategy, but I always proceeded with caution and did my best to mitigate the risk.

Continuously generating new ideas and choosing which ones to implement is an ongoing business strategy that's important to any company's success and growth. Keep in mind, you don't always need to come up with brand-new ideas. Sometimes, just a small, seemingly insignificant idea can lead to big things.

Here are five strategies to help you and your team continuously brainstorm fresh ideas:

- Host scheduled brainstorming sessions with a diverse team within your organization. Each session should have a specific focus, such as ways to improve marketing, strategies to enhance customer service, or developing concepts for new products/services.
- Pay attention to customer feedback. Seek inspiration from suggestions that are offered. An alternative is to host customer/client focus groups, or to send out a brief questionnaire encouraging people to submit ideas on how your company can improve its offerings.
- Focus on industry trends and what your competitors are doing. Then come up with ways to apply a trend or do something better than your competition.
- Come up with a new product or service on a limited basis and then test it with a small audience before rolling it out to the public.
- Use data analytics to spot new opportunities and then use artificial intelligence tools to help transform the data into viable ideas.

FOR AN ENTREPRENEUR, THERE'S NO SUCH THING AS A 40-HOUR WORK WEEK

You have to be fully dedicated to your business, believe in it, and plan to make personal sacrifices to see it succeed. However, you also need to be able to go home and shut down your work mindset.

My daughter Carol, who runs the day-to-day operations of Embree Elevator (now that I am semi-retired), lives next door. I see her almost every day after work. We never talk business when we're not in the office. After all, after a long work day, the last thing she wants to do is talk about work. I was the same way when I was working full time.

Learning how to manage your time, focus on the most important tasks of the moment, and delegating responsibilities when possible can help shorten a workday. However, I never found a foolproof formula that always worked, which meant putting in the long hours whenever it was necessary.

Virtually all entrepreneurs and business leaders have one thing in common—their workweek exceeds 40 hours. The extra time is needed to successfully manage the many responsibilities of a business operator.

Here are five strategies to help you make better use of your time as a business owner:

- Learn and implement time management techniques that meet your work habits and responsibilities.
- Become comfortable delegating responsibilities to people you trust. When possible, automate repetitive tasks, such as scheduling, invoicing, or creating social media content for your business. If necessary, you can hire freelance experts to handle certain tasks that take you a lot of time to handle, so you can free up your time to focus your efforts and attention where it's best utilized.
- Discover how to prioritize important tasks and responsibilities and handle those properly before investing the time to deal with less urgent items on your to-do list.
- Adopt the 80/20 rule (also known as the Pareto Principle). This means understanding that 80 percent of outcomes come from 20

percent of inputs. Identify the inputs that are most productive and make them a priority. For example, if you have certain clients or customers that generate the most revenue for your business, prioritize them first. It's about determining your best assets and using them to create maximum value.

- Each day, create a detailed to-do list, with each item on that list prioritized. Then, at the start of your day, focus on handling the three most important items at the top of your list.

THE CUSTOMER REALLY DOES ALWAYS COME FIRST

Without your clients or customers, you do not have a business. This makes them important. In fact, they should always be a top priority. The biggest benefits of keeping customers happy is the long-term relationships you build, and the positive word-of-mouth referrals that result from clients/customers being very happy with what you provide and how you provide it.

Meeting or exceeding your clients' wants, needs, and expectations should always remain a top priority. Make them feel special and cared about. Five strategies to help your business focus on keeping customers/clients happy include:

- Provide exceptional and highly personalized customer service.
- Listen to your customers/clients to determine each of their needs and expectations and customize your efforts accordingly by offering the right selection of products/services. By exceeding expectations, you're demonstrating that the customer/client is your priority.
- Based on what you learn from customer/client interactions, brainstorm ways to improve your product/service selection and the value they offer.
- Devise ways to build strong customer/client and brand loyalty. This will help you keep customers/clients longer, build stronger relationships, and generate positive word-of-mouth that can lead to new business. It's much easier and cost effective to generate repeat business and word-of-mouth referrals from existing

customers/clients than it is to seek out and land new customers/clients.

- Using a variety of methods, teach your customers/clients how to generate the best results or most value from using your products/services. Teach them how they can save time, save money, solve a problem they face, or achieve greater benefits from working with your business. This can be done through in-person interactions, publishing how-to articles in a newsletter or on a company website, offering instructional videos, or creating easy-to-understand and comprehensive manuals, for example.

BE ABLE TO ADAPT WHEN THINGS CHANGE SUDDENLY OR OVER TIME

Back in the day, in addition to maintaining and repairing elevators, we had our own machine shop, so we could build certain parts that we needed. The person we had running the machine shop could make anything. There came a time, however, when operating a machine shop was no longer economically beneficial, so we had to change our focus.

Making decisions to involve major changes in how a company does something is never easy. These decisions require additional thought and research, but they occasionally need to be made. And as the business owner, you're the person who ultimately needs to make those decisions. It's always nice when you can make important decisions within your own time frame, but that's not often possible. Sometimes, these decisions need to be made quickly to prevent or fix a time-sensitive problem.

Being able to adapt quickly as things change requires you, as the business operator, to stay informed. Be able to make educated predictions about the future based on past and current trends and reliable data.

The following strategies can help with this process:

- Maintain a flexible mindset. Be open to new ideas and avoid getting stuck in your current way of doing things.
- Continuously monitor up-and-coming trends, customer/client behaviors, competitor activities, and current news. Be on the

lookout for sudden shifts, whether it has to do with customer needs, economic trends, technological innovations, or industry-wide changes.

- Invest in learning and training opportunities for yourself and your employees.
- Use business systems that are reliable, scalable, and that support agility.
- During times of transition, keep your employees, customers/clients, suppliers, and all other necessary parties well informed. Be honest and transparent.

MAINTAIN FINANCIAL DISCIPLINE AND NEVER MAKE RASH MONEY DECISIONS

I'd like to say that making important financial decisions for a business is as easy as flipping a coin, but this is seldom the case. Throughout my professional career, I have always taken a conservative approach to spending, borrowing, and managing company funds. In fact, people say I can be very tight with money.

This attitude in part came from my wife, who was very frugal. She always wanted the best that money could buy but never wanted to overpay for it. As a business owner, I would always look for good deals, and avoid making rash financial decisions, especially when there was a lot of risk involved.

Here are a few key strategies to help prevent you from making rash decisions that could have negative financial repercussions to your business:

- Create a detailed budget and stick to it. However, reevaluate the budget on a regular basis to take into account growth and changes.
- Separate your emotions from your business-related spending, investments, and borrowing (taking on debt).
- Pay attention to real-time data related to cash flow, profit margins, expenses, etc., and look for unexpected changes, mistakes, or changing patterns.
- Develop a decision-making framework that you're comfortable

using on a consistent basis. It should take into account things like return on investment (ROI), risk level, and the alignment with your company's overall goals.
- Try to delay making important financial decisions or investments until you've had a chance to consider their ramifications with a clear head. In other words, try to avoid rash decisions related to anything having to do with finances. If necessary, consult with your accountant, banker, lawyer, business consultant, or others who are familiar with your company's finances.

ADOPT A CONSISTENT WORK ETHIC: STAY DISCIPLINED AND PERSISTENT

My work ethic has always been based on honesty with everyone I did business with. I was able to look people in the eye, and at the same time, look at myself in the mirror and know I was doing the right thing. My focus was on leading my life with integrity, transparency, and on following ethical business practices.

Developing a positive work ethic is something that happens over time. The following strategies can help you create and maintain a work ethic that will benefit you and your business:

- Each day, create a list of priorities. Then, identify and deal with the top three items on your list before getting sidetracked with other issues of the day.
- Develop a structured routine for yourself that fits your work style and responsibilities.
- Create accountability systems to ensure you stay focused on what's important and then lead by example.
- External accountability will help you maintain internal discipline.
- Use self-reflection as a tool to help you identify patterns, improve your habits, and stay focused on your goals.
- Try to eliminate the biggest time wasters in your daily schedule. Remove as many distractions as possible and then consider delegating tasks when necessary.

CREATE VALUE IN WHATEVER YOU DO

My goal was always to create value in whatever I did and leave things better than when I started. This was a philosophy I also insisted my employees follow, especially when they were working in the field. It might take more money or time to properly pursue this philosophy, but I have found that it's well worth it. It's something clients or customers notice and appreciate.

When one of my employees finished a project working for a client, I wanted them to be able to pat themselves on the back knowing they did more than what was expected. Depending on the type of business you're operating, this could mean many different things.

Here are some strategies that can help encourage you and your team to create value in whatever is being done:

- Have everyone on your team focus on problem solving, as opposed to simply completing a given task as quickly as possible.
- Figure out how to make every task align with your company's overall objectives.
- Foster a culture of teamwork and ownership among employees, so they're highly invested in the quality of the work they do.
- Find ways to streamline tasks while somehow improving the outcome. In some cases, this can be achieved with more specialized training, by implementing new technologies or software, or using the latest equipment.
- Promote teamwork and cross-functional collaboration, so employees share their knowledge and find ways to work together in a more productive way. One way I did this was to have veteran employees train new employees, and work with them as a mentor.

TAKE "CALCULATED RISKS" NOT "RISKS" WHENEVER POSSIBLE

I've talked a lot about this throughout the book. Risk taking is part of making decisions as a business owner. Whenever you make a decision, you want to base it on as much factual and up-to-date information as possible to lower the potential risk involved.

After evaluating the facts and data related to a risk, I always went with my gut instinct, which was based on my years of experience. Learn to trust your gut. If something does not feel right, there's probably a good reason for that.

Taking risks is part of what being an entrepreneur and business owner is all about. However, there are many proven strategies for reducing risk when making important business or financial decisions. Here are a few useful examples:

- Conduct thorough research to gather timely and accurate information. Never just guess about something. Be able to back up your decisions with facts.
- Run financial projections. Consider cash flow models, perform a break-even analysis, or do ROI estimations.
- Consult with trusted experts and advisors. Depending on the type of decision, reach out to your lawyer, accountant, banker, or someone who possesses specialized knowledge that could be useful to help you make an educated decision and reduce the risk involved.
- Establish and stick to your risk limits. This means understanding the level of risk you're comfortable taking that can prevent overexposure. Also preset spending limits for specific things that are controllable, such as rent/lease payments, advertising, new equipment purchases, travel, etc.
- Always have a contingency plan. If things do not go as planned, determine in advance how you'll deal with the miscalculation and reduce potential losses. Also, make sure whatever risks you wind up needed to take are in line with your company's strategic goals. I have always avoided actions that could generate a quick buck but result in financial uncertainty in the future.

BE RESILIENT AND STAY OPTIMISTIC, ESPECIALLY DURING DIFFICULT TIMES

Life is good. I can say this now based on many years of life experience, but it's something you probably need to learn for yourself. Every day is a good day, but some are definitely better than others. Focus on the good as much as you can, but do not simply ignore the bad stuff you may have to deal with.

For me, being resilient means staying focused on long-term objectives and being able to pick myself up and refocus when something does not go as planned. Optimism is an emotion that can be helpful when running a business.

Understand that everything goes in cycles. When there are good things happening, something bad will eventually occur, but there will then be something that's good on the horizon. There's no point in moping around when things do not go your way. Always keep trying to make things better instead of waiting around for things to get better by themselves. You have to take action if you want something better to happen.

While you always want to showcase an optimistic mentality, especially when it comes to managing employees and working with customers/clients, you don't want to deceive yourself into making bad decisions due to being over-optimistic instead of focusing on facts. Magical thinking seldom works in business.

Here are five strategies that can help you stay resilient and optimistic as you go through the daily ups and downs associated with being an entrepreneur or business leader:

- Remain focused on what you can control. Invest your energy and resources into making the best out of (or fixing) whatever situation you're in.
- Communicate openly and clearly with your team so everyone stays on the same page.
- Learn from setbacks so you can avoid making the same or similar mistakes multiple times.
- Determine ways to successfully manage your stress and anxiety and use those methods throughout the day. Mental self-care is essential for staying resilient when running a business.
- Celebrate small wins, milestones, and achievements. This can help boost everyone's morale and build positive momentum.

FINAL THOUGHTS...

When people think about elevators, the name that comes to mind is typically Otis Elevator, not Embree Elevator—especially for people outside of Eastern Massachusetts and Southern New Hampshire. I am more than okay with that.

Every day, more than 2.4 billion people around the world ride in an elevator. Just about every building or multi-level commercial property you step into now has at least one elevator. There is, and always has been, plenty of opportunity in the elevator industry, even for smaller, regional companies like mine.

While wanting to keep my company localized, I saw tremendous potential for ongoing prosperity in the elevator industry. My goal was never to take on Otis Elevator. I never had the urge to manage more than 44,000 employees, operate from more than 1,400 offices, or be responsible for keeping millions of elevators running smoothly in more than 200 countries.

By keeping things on a smaller scale, I built a company that's profitable and sustainable. And for decades, I really enjoyed running it. We started as a regional company that serviced large freight elevators, but in the 1980s and 1990s, we expanded our services to include inspecting, maintaining, and repairing passenger elevators, too.

By seeking out these new opportunities, and by keeping up-to-date on the latest technological advancements in elevators, Embree Elevator has enjoyed steady growth, while operating from a single, centrally located office in Woburn, Massachusetts. And as you know, today it's a family owned and operated business that now has three generations of family members working for it.

I am extremely proud of what I've accomplished personally and professionally, although like everyone else, my life has been filled with ups and downs. I've considered writing this book as being a good opportunity to serve as a mentor to you and a new generation of entrepreneurs and business leaders.

I also wanted to check off one more item from my personal bucket list—writing and publishing a book that could become part of my legacy. I sincerely hope I achieved both objectives.

The final piece of advice I'd like to end with is to do whatever is necessary (as long as it's legal and will not hurt anyone) to pursue happiness in both your personal and professional life. Find what you love doing and pursue it. But, while you're working hard to achieve your professional success, do not forgo personal happiness. For me, this meant having a close-knit and loving family, but every person is different.

Everyone defines success in their own way. Come up with your own definition of personal and professional success and then create a plan to achieve it. Stay focused on what you want and be willing to work very hard for it. And most importantly, be proud of all your accomplishments along the way.

Now, at age 95, I have achieved just about everything I wanted out of life. But, every day, I continue to discover new opportunities to continue enjoying what life has to offer. I seek out new experiences, spend quality time with family and friends, and cherish all of the people who have made my life so special. To each and every one of those people, I am forever grateful.

About The Author

JAMES F. COMLEY'S journey into the elevator industry began more than 70 years ago, following his service in the Navy. Starting as a mechanic's assistant, he developed a fascination with elevators' mechanical precision and their crucial role in modern infrastructure. In 1973, James and his wife, Virginia, purchased Embree Elevator, setting out to shape it into full-service elevator company. Under James's leadership, Embree Elevator developed into a thriving regional provider known for excellence in elevator maintenance and service.

An advocate for safety, James served for over two decades on the Massachusetts Board of Elevator Regulations and was appointed Chairman in 2006. His advocacy for safety standards and mentorship of younger professionals helped shape industry practices across the state. He is also co-founder of The Elevator Museum, a unique institution dedicated to elevator history preservation.

James's passion for preservation is also evident in his community outreach. He and Virginia restored the historic Elijah Stearns Mansion in Bedford, MA. The historic home, featured in *Architectural Digest* and admired throughout New England, reflects their shared dedication to historic houses and the stories they carry.

In 2011, James received the Ellis Island Medal of Honor, recognizing his lasting contributions to industry and community. He also endowed a significant scholarship at the University of Massachusetts Lowell, supporting future innovators and tradespeople.

He lives in Bedford, MA, where he enjoys time with his family and friends.

Acknowledgments

I WOULD FIRST like to acknowledge my best friend, life partner, business partner, and beloved wife, Virginia Comley. Ginny was the love of my life. We shared every one of life's ups and downs, and I remain deeply proud and grateful for the remarkable journey we built together.

I am forever grateful to my daughter, Carol Washer, for stepping forward to lead Embree Elevator. Carol began her studies to become a registered nurse at Northeastern University, but in 1984, she made the selfless decision to change course and help guide Embree's future. Carol and her husband, Cliff, are my designated successors, and I could not be prouder of the leadership, integrity, and dedication they bring to the company.

My heartfelt thanks go to my family, especially my parents, John Ridgway Comley, Jr., and Freda Comley; my brother, John R. Comley, III; and my sister, Lois Comley Hamilton.

I am profoundly grateful for my children: Michael Comley, Bonnie Comley, Stephen Comley, and Carol Washer. I also thank my children-in-law, Clifford Washer, Stewart F. Lane, and Stephanie Comley, and my cherished grandchildren: Alex Washer, James Washer, Kristina Washer, Travis Comley, Jake Comley, Leah Lane, Lenny Lane, and Frankie Lane. My gratitude extends as well to my step-grandchildren, Eliana Lane and Harlyn Lane, and my step-great-grandchildren, Penny Rinkosk Lane and Asher Rinkoski Lane. Each of you has brought immeasurable joy and pride into my life.

I would also like to recognize my many mentors and colleagues from the US Navy, the International Union of Elevator Constructors (IUEC), David Morgan, and everyone at the Elevator Industry Educational Program (NEIEP). I am deeply appreciative of the friends and colleagues who helped create what is now known as the Elevator Museum at NEIEP. Special thanks to my son, Stephen Comley, who devoted countless hours to assembling, cataloging, and curating thousands of parts, brochures, and artifacts to "preserve the past and elevate the future." I also acknowledge Patrick Carrajat, founder of the Elevator Historical Society, whose vision and groundwork inspired the current Elevator Museum.

I am grateful for my partnership with John McHugh, my mentorship with Charlie Murphy, and for all the employees of Embree Elevator, past and present, especially Henry Embree, Kenneth Embree, David S. Lucey, Michael Caron, Scott E. Hult, Michael S. Lucey, Gary Sawyer, Lucas Vatcher, Sandie Fay, Donna Picardi, Daniel Garofalo, Paul Marzeotti, Delaney Tivnan, and Joseph Rizzo whose commitment and craftsmanship have defined the company's legacy.

Finally, I thank the entire elevator industry community, whose dedication to safety in the installation, modernization, and maintenance of elevators, escalators, and moving walkways protects millions of people every day.

My sincere appreciation to my publishers, Jennifer Dorsey and Vanessa Campos, at the Broad Book Group, and to Jason Rich, the true writer, who transformed my thoughts, stories, and advice into what I hope is a concise, encouraging, and meaningful book.

www.ingramcontent.com/pod-product-compliance
Lightning Source LLC
LaVergne TN
LVHW052341100826
845147LV00021B/1140

9781963549386